Creating Mystery Parties for Kids
with a focus on S.T.E.M. and learning

By: Joseph J. Franco

Copyright 2021 by Joseph J. Franco

Illustrations Copyright 2021 by Joseph J. Franco

All rights reserved

Printed in the United States of America

For everyone who said
"Hey, you should do a book for kids now"

Table of Contents

Introduction	1
Problem Solving	3
Getting Started	5
Learning Guidelines & Objectives	7
Kindergarten (Ages 5-6)	8
First Grade (Ages 6-7)	10
Second Grade (Ages 7-8)	12
Third Grade (Ages 8-9)	14
Fourth Grade (Ages 9-10)	16
Fifth Grade (Ages 10-11)	18
All Grade Levels	20
Clue Creation Examples	22
Generating Story Ideas	28
Difference Between Puzzles and Clues	30
Game Set Up	33
Game Play & Design	35
Game Help	38
Timing	40
Keeping Kids Involved	42
Game Ending	43
Advance Game Play	44

Halloween Ghost
Sample Game One Ages 2-5   45

Trail of the Vampire
Sample Game Two Ages 3-6   49

Pirates Treasure
Sample Game Three Ages 4+   51

Zombie Hunt
Sample Game Four Ages 5+   56

Ghostly Treasure
Sample Game Five Ages 6+   61

Haunted House
Sample Game Six Ages 7+   71

Witches & Warlocks
Sample Game Seven Ages 8+   79

Who or What?
Sample Game Eight Ages 9+   85

Seed Ideas   91

Wrapping Up and Moving Forward   95

Introduction

Since the success of my first book, *How to Create Your Own Murder Mystery Party,* there have been fifteen more fun and successful parties. Lots of murder, blood, adult situations, and gruesome scenes filled our parties, which really could go on until, as the invitation stated, "??". Sometimes ending with a horror movie marathon until everyone just passed out from exhaustion or 'over consumption'.

As nature took its course and our carefree lifestyle came to an end, one question kept popping up more and more from our guests "Can we bring our kids?" For us, a similar question, what do we do with our kids during the party?

Initially, the infant stage was more of a logistics problem. Where can we put them down to sleep, where can we feed them, keep them away from noise, etc.? This had an obvious effect on the party dynamics for a while, as the parents would, rightfully so, be more concerned with their children than who stole the 1000-year-old jewel encrusted skull and killed the museum curator.

We then came to realize that the parties became more of a time for parents to gather, socialize, take a break from the rigors of parenting, and try to solve a puzzle or two just for fun. Because of this, single friends and couples without kids were able to complete and solve the mystery without too much competition.

I began experimenting with various ways to incorporate the young children into the party. Typically, this was merely a way to have them out and about. Some of them would have a clue, be wearing a clue, or be an actual clue. At times, we also asked the parents to put them in a certain costume or be a type of character. This worked for a little while and did add a fun dynamic to the parties. For this to work I had to make the parties much less complex and much shorter, still fun, but nothing like the original parties that took a few hours to complete.

As the kids grew and became more active, I had to follow suit with other ideas. Sometimes this would be creating activities to keep them busy, such as Halloween games, puzzles, etc. Again, this did work, but I realized I was just stalling. It was obvious what had to be done. I was going to have to incorporate them into the party completely or have two separate parties, one for kids and one for adults that can get babysitters.

Once the kids got a little older, they became more conscious of what was going on and wanted to be more involved in solving the mystery. It was time to experiment with the two options, combined and separate.

For the combined parties, I kept in mind the ages that would be attending. I did things more along the lines of space aliens and witches as opposed to decapitations and bloodletting. I would create the parties for the adults, keeping in mind puzzles and clues that the kids could either solve on their own or help their parents by finding items needed to keep the party moving forward. This worked well with kids under 4 or 5.

Over the years different variations of the above were tried. Below are some options to mix and match:

- Have the kids' mystery party earlier in the evening, then have the kids go play on their own, while adults enjoy their party.

- Adults chip in for a babysitter/s to hang-out with the kids at an alternate location.

- Run the two mysteries at the same time and decide during game development if I want them to actually be related to each other or have some cross-over/merge point. This proved to be way too much work!

- Have the kids party on a different day and parents just need to find a babysitter on their own to attend the adult party. This is what I eventually settled on and how it works till this day.

Most likely you will need to make the transition in a similar manner if you are new parents or the majority of your guests are. You can first have the kids play along with their parents for a year or two with the combined parties. Once the kids are old enough, or you are ready to give it a shot, then host a mystery party just for the kids.

Of course, these kids' mystery parties can be done for just about any other occasion. We have done them as birthday parties, sleepovers, etc. In the end, as always, it is about having fun and if you can sneak in some educational components, why not. This focus point is where will begin.

Problem Solving

There are some terms that I want to discuss that are all a part of why these parties are beneficial to kids.

There are typically three ways things can be learned: Analytical, Visual, and Hands-on. Let's take the slope of a line as an example. Analytically this would be the equation: Slope = $\Delta y/\Delta x$
Visually it would look like this:

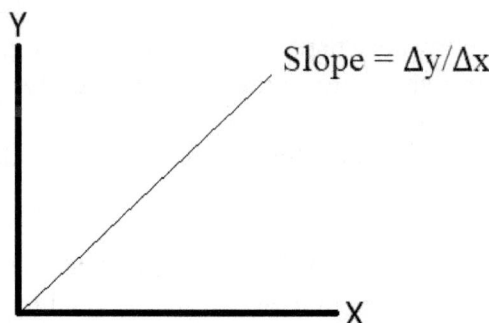

Hands on would be doing a drawing of the line on graph paper. Ultimately the best way to learn is to combine all three of these techniques, but depending on the way a person's brain is set up, different people will process each of these differently and will prefer one way to learn over the others. To be able to utilize any of these learning techniques, a person needs to be able to process information; this is where we transition to being able to learn.

Critical thinking is typically defined in a few ways, but in general it is the process/ability to take in information and actively and skillfully conceptualize, apply, analyze, synthesize, and evaluate information. This information is attained or generated through observation, experimentation, experience, reflection, reasoning, and communication. Once this process is complete, it will lead you to an idea on which you can take action or make a decision.

For something to be logical or a logical step taken, the previous step must be true to move on to the next step; this is logical processing. Critical thinking and logical processing are all part of the learned skill of problem solving.

Just as research has shown that our bodies need exercise, the same holds true for our brains. Professional athletes spend a lot of time training their bodies to be skilled at a particular sport. There typically is a big difference between, for example, an amateur golfer and a professional golfer. One has practiced and trained a lot more than the other. If the amateur was placed against the pro, the typical outcome is obvious.

The same holds true for problem solving - the more you practice and train, the better you become at using critical thinking and logical processing to solve problems.

Getting kids into the practice of using their brains to solve problems and learning how to do so, along with what works best for them at an early age, is what I feel should be a major goal of every parent. This will put them on a path of educational enlightenment that will continue into their adult life.

Getting Started

One of the big factors when coming up with a kid's mystery party is the ages and abilities of the kids. In other words, what realistically can the kids do and solve, and, at the same time have fun? Chances are, you will also have kids of various ages playing the game at the same time, this needs to be factored in as well.

I decided early on I would make these parties a learning opportunity. Currently working as an educator had a lot to do with that. The most recent parties I have thrown for the kids have all worked out great. The kids are having too much fun to even realize they are learning.

Having a master's degree in engineering and over 14 years teaching experience gives me a slight advantage in the experience category, but creativity is limitless, and the learning objectives discussed later will help greatly with focusing in on the learning part.

Since my background is engineering, I wanted to focus on S.T.E.M., which is the current buzz acronym. This also is a big pet peeve of mine that I am going to take advantage of your attention to explain why, bear with me while I step up on my soap box.

Being an engineer, STEM strikes me as a very silly acronym, that most likely was created by a non-'STEM' person. STEM, if you don't already know, stands for Science, Technology, Engineering and Math. While it is fantastic that people are trying to focus on these important topics in the education system (amazing that they are not the primary …), it also shows that the general population does not understand what engineering actually is. I know people would be more likely to buy a book stating, "with a focus on S.T.E.M. and learning" as opposed to "with a focus on Engineering and learning". STEM is in the public eye. Engineers use science, technology and math to solve, create, etc. Engineering IS the combination of Science, Technology and Math. If you want to get kids to study/focus on STM, teach Engineering. You can do STM without doing Engineering, you cannot do Engineering without STM. S.T.E.M. therefor it is an oxymoron. You have all these classes, programs, etc. popping up using the STEM acronym. Again, great to promote all the disciplines, as Science, Math, Technology and Engineering are all critical areas, but all you needed to do was promote ENGINEERING and you would cover all the rest. I feel that STEM, in a way, is helping to confuse what the heart of engineering is. Engineering = STM. I am going to skip the S.T.E.A.M (addition of Art) and the S.T.E.A.M.M (addition of Art and Music) movements for another book, I'll now step off my soap box and get back to the topic at hand, mystery parties.

Kids need constant activity. The younger the child the less time they will want to sit and actually try to 'solve' a problem. You are going to want to keep them up, active, and engaged. At times, kids may need to be broken into groups to work on a specific task, then brought back together. If you have shy kids, you may need to give them a specific objective or 'assign' another kid as a team mate to work on a task, then re-join the main group later. Even in the example parties later in this book, there are simple ways to modify the parties for different groups, sizes, ages, etc.

Every state and county have learning guidelines/objectives for each grade level. If you choose not to use the ones listed here, you can search the internet and you should be able to find your locations' specific guidelines pretty easily. You can even call you child's school and ask for them. These are indicators/expectations of a child's abilities at certain age and grade level. They can easily be incorporated into a mystery game as puzzles, clues, goals, etc. The next pages cover a large number of examples for you to use as a resource and baseline. There is more than enough here to keep you going for a long while.

Learning Guidelines & Objectives

On the following pages you will find target learning guidelines and objectives for a few of the national grade levels. Besides common sense and what you feel your child should know and be able to do at a certain age and grade level, these are general state standards to use for reference. If you do a search on "grade level expectations" or "standards of learning" on your state education website, you should find lists you can follow that are specific to your school district.

A number of these main subjects are broken down into detailed objectives early on. Math, for example, as you will see below, is broken down into such items as "Can name/ID squares, triangles, circles, and rectangles, Match numerals, zero to ten, to a correct number of dots or shapes." This is also done with Science, Literacy, etc.

Starting in third grade, these same topics (Math, Science, Literacy, etc.) become a little more generalized and you can then combine subjects. Math and Science for example can be combined into one game clue or challenge so it covers both topics.

For most of these guidelines it should be pretty easy to create clues and challenges that exercise these standards. By no means are these complete and/or comprehensive. Objectives can be expanded and reduced to fit your needs. I have narrowed down a good portion of them simply because they are more abstract concepts that do not lend themselves well to the goal of these mystery style games. I have also simplified a number of them, as to make them easier to apply to the clues or puzzles.

A child in fifth grade should be able to do all the things a child in first grade can do. As we get to higher grade levels, I focus on more items specific to those grades levels and assume items from lower grades are known. Of course, you can incorporate lower grade level items if desired. You can even create clue steps, going from easy to hard. All of this can be incorporated into the mystery.

Following these guidelines while creating your mystery party will help in creating clues and challenges, while appropriately challenging the children playing your game. These challenges will either exercise their brains or help them learn something new. Simply changing the wording on a number of learning objectives can turn them into clues and challenges.

It is also very easy to take a simple learning objective that you like, for example:

"Can name/ID squares, triangles, circles, and rectangles"

and increase its complexity for older kids to:

"Can name/ID 3D objects cubes, pyramids, sphere, and cuboids".

As stated earlier, I left some objectives out. If they can measure length in the first grade, they should be able to do it in the third grade.

Kindergarten (Ages 5-6)

Math

- Can name/ID squares, triangles, circles, and rectangles.
- Match numerals, zero to ten, to a correct number of dots or shapes
- Count objects using one to one correspondence.
- Model "adding to" and "taking away" using objects.
- Sort a group of objects using one or two common attributes.
- Describes the position of objects in relation to other objects and themselves using the words: over/under, top/bottom, etc. relative to open space.
- Recognizes and copy simple patterns with objects and symbols.
- Measures length and weight using both non-standard units and appropriate tools, such as a give shape.
- Uses words that describe time and what comes first based on a sequence of events.

Science

- Describing the effects of hot and cold on materials.
- Distinguish between living and non-living things.
- Pair adult/baby animal pictures.

Literacy

- Identifies words with the same beginning or ending sounds.
- Make up own rhymes given a situation or event.
- Identifies the first letter of their first name when written.
- Can recognize first name when written.

History

- Identifies examples of past events and people in legends, stories, and historical milestones. Examples: George Washington, James West, Ben Franklin, etc.
- Identifies the people and events honored by the holidays of Thanksgiving Day, Presidents' Day, Independence Day, etc.

Economics

- Match descriptions of work that people do with the names of those jobs. Construction Worker, Teacher, Scientist, Engineer, Fireman, etc.

Geography

- Describe the relative location of people or an object by using positional words, with emphasis on near/far, above/below, left/right, and behind/in front.
- Use simple maps and globes to develop situational awareness.
- Be able to locate things located on a map and on a globe model of the Earth. Possibly incorporate electronic maps as well.

Fine Arts

- Sing, play, or move at the appropriate time following a vocal/instrumental introduction.
- Match movement to rhythmic dance patterns.
- Use movement to enhance music, stories, and poems.
- Perform dances and games from various/other cultures.
- Identify common instruments by sight and sound.
- Identify men's, women's, and children's voices.

First Grade (Ages 6-7)

Math

- Solve one-step story and picture problems using basic addition of facts.
- Count and write numbers from 0 to 100.
- Group a collection of objects into tens and ones.
- Count forward by ones, twos, fives, and tens
- Identify and write the parts of a set that represent fractions for halves, thirds, and fourths.
- Identify the number of pennies equivalent to a nickel, a dime, and a quarter.
- Determine the value of a collection of coins and bills.
- Tell time to the half-hour, using analog and digital clocks.
- Measure length, weight/mass, and volume.
- Know and use calendar vocabulary months, today, yesterday, next week, last week, years, etc.
- Identify and triangle, square, rectangle, and circle according to number of sides, vertices, and right angles.
- Investigate, identify or describe various forms of data collection (examples: recording daily temperature, favorite cookies, ice cream flavor, colors) using tables, picture graphs, and object graphs.
- Interpret information displayed in a picture or object graph, using the vocabulary, more, less, fewer, greater than, less than, and equal to.
- Sort and classify objects according to one or more attributes, including color, size, shape, and thickness.
- Recognize a wide variety of growing and repeating patterns.
- Demonstrate an understanding of equality through the use of the equal sign.

Science

- Conduct simple experiments to answer questions or verify an assumption.
- Observe differences in physical properties using the senses (smell, taste, touch, etc.).

- Use simple tools to enhance observations/investigations (magnifying glass, binoculars, etc.).
- Classified and arrange objects according to attributes or properties.
- Items are measured using length, mass, and volume.
- Show some liquids will separate when mixed with water, but others will not.
- Show some common solids will dissolve in water (hot/cold), but others will not.
- Anatomy of plants, which include trees.
- Plants need food, air, water, light, and a place to grow.
- Physical characteristics (body coverings, body shape, appendages, and methods of movement).
- The sun is the source of heat and light that warms the land, air, and water.
- Night and day are caused by the rotation of the Earth.

Literacy

- Sort items alphabetically by first letter.
- Ask and answer who, what, when, where, why, and how questions about a story line.
- Identify characters, settings, and important traits in a story.

Second Grade (Ages 7-8)

Math

- Identify the parts of a set represent fractions for halves, thirds, fourths, sixths, eighths, and tenths.
- Recognize even and odd numbers.
- Identify the place value of each digit in a three-digit numeral.
- Round two-digit numbers to the nearest tenth.
- Count by twos, fives, and tens, starting at various multiples of 2, 5, or 10.
- Solve one- and two-step addition and subtraction problems, using data (clues) from simple tables, picture graphs, and bar graphs.
- Count a collection of various coins whose total value is $7.15.
- Measure, length to the nearest centimeter and inch.
- Weigh the mass of objects in pounds/ounces and kilograms/grams.
- Measure liquid volume in cups, pints, quarts, gallons, and liters.
- Tell and write time to the nearest five minutes, using analog and digital clocks. Note: Most of my high school students have problems reading analog clocks ...
- Read the temperature on a Celsius and/or Fahrenheit thermometer to the nearest 10 degrees.
- Compare circles/spheres, squares/cubes, and rectangles/rectangular prisms.
- Solve problems by completing numerical sentences involving the basic facts for addition and subtraction.
- Solve story problems, using the numerical sentences.

Science

- Take measurements of length, volume, mass, and temperature in metric units (centimeters, meters, liters, degrees Celsius, grams, kilograms) and imperial units (inches, feet, yards, cups, pints, quarts, gallons, degrees Fahrenheit, ounces, pounds).
- Pictures and bar graphs are constructed using numbered axes.
- Unexpected or unusual quantitative data/clues are recognized and put into a logical pattern.
- Investigate and understand that natural and artificial magnets have certain characteristics and attract specific types of metals.

- Understand the physical difference between natural and artificial magnets.
- Understand law of poles (magnets attract and repel each other).
- Use and understand the magnetic compass and why it works.
- Investigate basic properties of solids, liquids, and gases.
- Understand concepts that include mass, volume.
- Discuss the processes of changes in matter from one state to another (condensation, evaporation, melting, and freezing).
- Understand that plants and animals undergo a series of orderly changes in their life cycles (frogs, butterflies, fruit).
- Understand basic types, changes, and patterns of weather (Temperature, wind, precipitation).
- Understand that weather and seasonal changes affect plants, animals, and their surroundings (migration, hibernation, camouflage, adaptation, dormancy).
- Understand planetary environmental changes impact all plant and animal cycles.
- Understand that plants produce oxygen and food, are a source of useful products, and provide benefits in nature. Availability of plant products (fiber, cotton, oil, spices, lumber, rubber, medicines, and paper) affects the development of a geographic area. Plants provide homes and food for many animals. Roots prevent soil from washing away/mudslides.

Third Grade (Ages 8-9)

Math

- Read, write, and identify the place and value of each digit in a six-digit whole number, with and without models.
- Round whole numbers, 9,999 or less, to the nearest ten, hundred, and thousand.
- Compare and order whole numbers, each 9,999 or less.
- Name and write fractions and mixed numbers represented by a model or visual aid.
- Represent fractions and mixed numbers with models and symbols.
- Compare fractions having like and unlike denominators, using words and symbols (>, <, =, or ≠), with models.
- Estimate and determine the sum or difference of two whole numbers.
- Create and solve single-step and multistep practical problems involving sums or differences of two whole numbers, each 9,999 or less.
- Represent multiplication and division through 10 × 10, using a variety of approaches and models.
- Create and solve single-step practical problems that involve multiplication and division through 10 x 10.
- Demonstrate fluency with multiplication facts of 0, 1, 2, 5, and 10.
- Solve single-step practical problems involving multiplication of whole numbers, where one factor is 99 or less and the second factor is 5 or less.
- Determine the value of a collection of bills and coins whose total value is $5.76 or less.
- Compare the value of two sets of coins or two sets of coins and bills.
- Make change from $5.76 or less using a variety of coins and bills.
- Measure length to the nearest ½ inch, inch, foot, yard, centimeter, and meter.
- Measure liquid volume in cups, pints, quarts, gallons, and liters.

- Measure the distance around simple geometric shapes in order to determine its perimeter using Imperial and metric units.
- Tell time to the nearest minute, using analog and digital clocks. Focus should be on analog.
- Solve practical problems related to elapsed time in one-hour increments within a 12-hour period.
- The student will read temperature to the nearest degree.
- Verify and read data represented pictographs or bar graphs.

Science

- Natural (night/day/seasons) events are sequenced chronologically.
- Length, volume, mass, and temperature are estimated and measured in metric and Imperial units.
- Time is measured to the nearest minute.
- Purpose, function and examples of the 6 simple machines. Possibly can include use of.
- The physical properties of an object remain the same as the material is changed in visible size.
- Animal life cycles and plant life cycles.
- Understand the relationships among organisms and the concept of food chains.
- Understand the difference and roll of herbivore, carnivore, omnivore predator and prey in the food chain.
- Simple phases of the moon and effects on tides (gravitational pull)
- Understand the water cycle and its relationship to life on Earth.
- Understand energy from the sun, sources of renewable and energy and nonrenewable energy.

History & Geography

- Influence of Rome, Greece, and Africa on the present world in terms of architecture, government, tradition and sports.
- Develop map skills by positioning and labeling the seven continents and five oceans to create a world map.
- Exploration of the Americas by Christopher Columbus, Juan Ponce de León, Jacques Cartier, Christopher Newport, Vikings.

- Develop map skills by locating past or present European and African locations on a map.
- Locating local historical places or more general regions in the Americas explored by Christopher Columbus (San Salvador in the Bahamas), Juan Ponce de León (near St. Augustine, Florida), Jacques Cartier (near Quebec, Canada), and Christopher Newport (Jamestown, Virginia)
- Understand and demonstrate the concept of trade when people and regions cannot produce everything they need, they specialize in what they can make and trade for the rest.

Fourth Grade (Ages 9-10)

Math

- Identify the place value for each digit in whole numbers expressed through millions.
- Compare whole numbers using symbols ($>, <, \leq \geq$ and $=$).
- Round whole numbers to the nearest thousand, ten thousand, and hundred thousand.
- Given a model or graphics, write the decimal and fraction equivalents.
- Estimate and measure liquid volume and describe the results in U.S. customary units (cups, pints, quarts, etc.)
- Describe and use lines, line segments, angles, including endpoints, and vertices.
- Identify lines that illustrate intersection, parallelism, and perpendicularity.
- Demonstrate congruence of plane figures after geometric transformations, such as reflection, translation, and rotation, using mirrors, paper folding, and tracing.
- Recognize the images of figures resulting from geometric transformations, such as translation, reflection, and rotation, including 3D.
- Organize, display, and interpret data from a variety of graphs from collected data.

Science

- Appropriate instruments are selected and used to measure length, mass, volume, temperature and time in metric or imperial units.
- Data/Evidence is collected, recorded, analyzed, and displayed using bar and basic line graphs.
- Data/Evidence are given with simple graphs, pictures, written statements, and numbers.
- Know that an objects motion is described by its direction and speed.
- Objects can have potential and kinetic energy.
- Force on objects can translate to motion and this motion can be opposed by friction.
- Understand basic electricity and circuits. Example: The operation and/or construction of a battery, wires, switch and light or motor.
- Energy can be transformed into light and motion and heat.
- Construct a simple electromagnet.
- Understand the concept of magnets and magnetism.
- Concept of insulators and conductors.
- Plant anatomy, structure, and life cycle.
- Impact of humans on the ecosystem.
- Appropriate meteorological tools are used to measure weather.
- Understand weather phenomena and cycles.
- Name planets and their order in the solar system.
- Understand relative sizes of planets and sun (our star).
- Understand relationship between universe, galaxy, and solar system.
- Understand the difference between asteroids, comets, meteors and meteorites.
- Understand the motions of the planets relative to seasons and time of day.
- Understand moon phases and the mechanism of an eclipse.
- Investigate minerals and rocks.
- Understand use of natural resources for energy.

Fifth Grade (Ages 10-11)

Math

- Identify prime and composite numbers.
- Convert fractions to decimals.
- Round decimal numbers to nearest whole numbers.
- Understand and sort/organize odd and even numbers.
- Understand and use the concepts of perimeter, area and volume.
- Be able to measure perimeter, area and volume in given units.
- Identify the properties of a circle. (diameter, radius, chord and circumference).
- Identify triangles (right, acute, obtuse, equilateral, isosceles and scalene).
- Be able to identify right, acute, obtuse and straight angles.
- Identify 2D plane geometric shapes, square, rectangle, parallelogram, rhombus, triangle and trapezoid.
- Identify 3D objects cubes, pyramids, sphere, and cuboids.
- Be able to solve single, as well as multistep practical problems involving addition, subtraction, multiplication and division.
- Given data, be able to plot line graphs.

Science

- Investigate the creation and transmission of sound through air (a gas), solids, and fluids.
- Identify the difference between frequency and amplitude and how it applies to sound.
- Through experimentation, investigate the visible spectrum through prism refraction.
- Through experimentation, investigate light reflection, refractions and basic optics with lenses and water. Small laser pointers and mirrors is an option.
- Understand the four phases of matter, solid, liquid, gas and plasma.
- Understand the properties associated with phases of matter.
- Investigate the effects of temperature on matter.
- Understand atoms and molecules are the foundation of matter.
- Investigate mixtures and solutions.
- Understand basic cell structure and function.

- Classify organisms using physical characteristics.
- Identify traits that enable organisms to survive in their environments.
- Investigate and categorize/identify rocks and minerals.
- Understand geological, ecological, and physical characters of ocean and terrestrial structures.
- Understand the process of fossil formation.
- Understand earth's interior and surface structure.
- Understand plate tectonics, weathering, erosion, and volcanic action and how these change the planet.
- Understand human impact on the planet.

All Grade Levels

School systems guidelines/objectives listed below vary greatly because of a number of factors. Some children take music and/or dance early in their lives, so their skill set will be higher than those that did not. Same is true for technology and engineering. I've had students come into High School having no idea how to use a tape measure, never built a model or used a tool. Over the years I have noticed this getting worse and worse. Objectives can be used for investigation, creation, research, etc. Because of this, these are general guidelines and again can be farmed for ideas. These guidelines range from basic to advanced.

Music and Dance

- Be able to follow and repeat simple dance steps and patterns.
- Be able to create and sing rhymes based on a given subject or items.
- Read and perform music on a preferred instrument.
- Echo and notate music.
- Sing selected short songs or selected lines of music.
- Define and use music terminology.
- Identify instruments by sound.

Technology and Engineering

- Properly use a ruler and tape measure.
- Identify and use basic tools including flat and Phillips screw drivers, hammer, saw, slip-joint, diagonal cutting and needle nose pliers, vise grips, ratchets and wrenches.
- Understand the meaning of technology and its impact on society.
- Understand the difference between a scientist, technician and engineer.
- Sketch an idea on paper that can be understood by others without them present.
- Demonstrate the understanding of basic structures.
- Demonstrate the understanding of forces, including friction.
- Understand and use the six simple machines.

- Understand and be able to solve gear problems and puzzles.
- Demonstrate the center of gravity in relation to the balance of objects.
- Understand the forces acting on an aircraft, lift, drag, gravity and thrust.
- Demonstrate converting binary to decimal and vice-versa.
- Demonstrate how to assemble a simple circuit.
- Demonstrate how to solve a problem with a simple circuit.
- Demonstrate simple coding logic.
- Demonstrate ways to create sound waves.
- Understand propagation of sound waves through fluids and solids.
- Demonstrate reflection and angles using laser pointers.
- Use technology to solve a clue, camera, tablet, etc.

You can expand this into health, for example using first aid techniques on an 'injured' person involved in the story line. Crime scene investigation, local history, computers, etc., all can be incorporated into the story. Use what you know to create scenarios and learning situations to relay the information to the kids while they are having a good time.

Clue Creation Examples

There are infinite ways of developing clues from the prompts above. Below are some examples that range from basic to advanced, based on the prompts from the 'Music and Dance' and 'Technology and Engineering' baseline. Here is where your creativity can shine. During the creation of your mystery party, you will integrate each of these clues within the storyline. These are just examples and not related to any of the example games later in the book.

- Learn to properly use a ruler and tape measure.

There are four magic staffs that the wizard can use. Each one has its own magic power based on its size. Be careful not to attempt a spell using the wrong staff!

Staff of Silence is 6" long
Staff of Slowness is 8" long
Staff of Sitting is 11 ½" long
Staff of Running is 12" long

- Tell time to the nearest minute, using analog and digital clocks.

Players can match clues based on time presented in both analog and digital. Believe it or not, a good portion of my high school students do not know how to read an analog clock ...

- Demonstrate simple coding logic.

This one is a much more advanced version of a clue you can put in a game. I will be using this clue once my players get to high school age.

The scientist has left a single hint in the code below that will generate an error. The error is an alphabet letter that is the first clue for the name of the suspected thief.

```c
#include <stdio.h>
int main()
{
    int firstNumber, secondNumber, sumOfTwoNumbers;

    printf("Enter two integers: ");

    // Two integers entered by user is stored using scanf() function
    scanf("%d %d", &firstNumber, &secondNumber);

    // sum of two numbers is stored in variable sumOfTwoNumbers
    sumOfTwoNumbers = firstNumber + secondNumber;

    // Displays sum
    printf("%d + %d = %d", firstNumber, secondNNumber, sumOfTwoNumbers);

    return 0;
}
```

Answer: N

- Identify and use basic tools including flat and Phillips screw drivers, hammer, saw, slip-joint, diagonal cutting and needle nose pliers, vise grips, ratchets and wrenches.

During game play, a box (treasure, clue, magic, etc.) can be 'locked'. Players would need to use tools that can be found during the game to open the box.

- Demonstrate how to assemble a simple circuit.

or

- Demonstrate how to solve a problem with a simple circuit.

Supplies from any basic electronics kit can be used to create any basic circuit, even something as simple as a battery and a light.

In your created story line, the players need to create a simple circuit to emit light, sound, etc. or maybe they need to do the opposite, and 'defuse' a bomb. For the assembly idea, in its simplest form you would need:

- Battery
- Wires
- Mini-bulb

Players can find the items and assemble the working circuit.

You can even supply printed out versions of these components to simulate the circuit and just check if the players have done it correctly.

Here is a quick example I did using an online circuit design program.

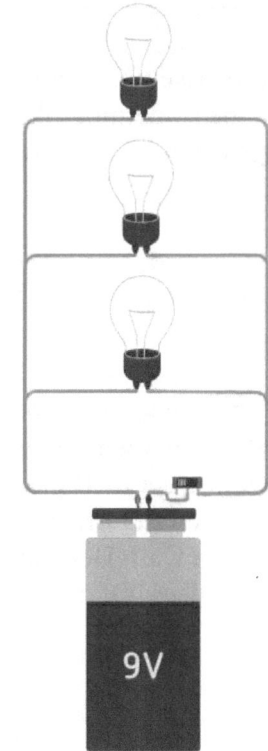

Basic: If the above circuit is turned on will all three lights come on?
Answer: Yes

Advanced: If all three lights are on and the middle bulb is removed, what will happen to the other two bulbs?
Answer: They will stay on.

- Demonstrate reflection and angles using laser pointers.

This puzzle type was incorporated into one of my adult parties years ago. I used a series of mirrors (cheap compacts from $1 store) that had to be placed at specific locations and angles based on clues, as well as a small laser pointer, also placed at a specific location and angle. If all this was done correctly the laser would 'point' to a specific location revealing a major clue.

You can also have the players assemble items for a mad scientist type of story line. A set up could be something like this. "The scientist has been sending secret messages using the following items:

- A tin can or paper tube
- Aluminum Foil or Mylar
- Tape
- Laser pointer.

If you use the tin can both ends need to be open. The aluminum foil or Mylar needs to be stretched tightly over the opening of one end of the tube or can and held in place with tape. If the players then speak or sing into the tube while reflecting the laser off the reflective surface figures and shapes will be reflected to a wall. Depending on the laser, you can do this at very impressive distances. Of course, be careful of eyes when using a laser pointer.

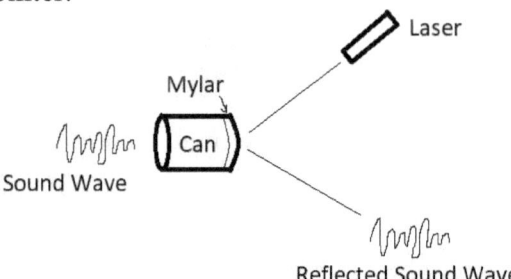

- Identify instruments by sound.

Someone found a recording, that could possibly be the criminal, playing a song. If the players can identify the instrument, then find someone who knows how to play that instrument, that might narrow down the suspects.

- Read and perform music on a preferred instrument.

You can use musical clues, such as the one below that spells out 'BAG' in treble clef notes.

- Demonstrate converting binary to decimal and vice-versa.

You can set up a very simple puzzle for the players in this type of scenario. Have a conversion key, such as:

3	5	7	9	11	13	15
U	B	C	D	E	F	G

2	4	6	8	10	12	14
R	I	J	K	O	M	N

The previous would be something the players can find. The following is the binary code that would need to be decoded using the previous key.

This can be written in a journal, scrolled on a wall, etc.

Binary code is as follows:

64	32	16	8	4	2	1

If you put 1110 into the above table as follows, then add the top numbers you will get 14.

64	32	16	8	4	2	1
			1	1	1	0

8+4+2+0 = 14

In binary 11 = 3, 1110 = 14, 1001 = 9, etc.

11-1110-1001-1011-10 10-1010-111-1000

This will decode to "Under Rock"

Generating Story Ideas

Generating story ideas can be fun. You can come up with a bunch looking over ghost stories, history, classic mysteries, etc.

A few simple story line examples:

- Treasure Hunt
- Alien Invasion.
- Monster (Vampire, Werewolf, etc.) Hunter
- Mad Scientist
- Haunted House

If you look at that small list and brainstorm for a little while, I am sure ideas will start coming to you. A few of the example games are based on the initial story lines above. This might help you see how you can go from an idea to a fully developed party and the incorporation of the clues and puzzles.

Once you have your story line, it is time to decide what exactly the learning objectives of the party and goals of the players will be. Will the players be working as a team for a goal, in multiple teams, working against each other, etc.?

As previously stated, kids' imaginations are very expansive, open, and forgiving (usually!). Brainstorming ideas for kid's parties, in my opinion, is much easier than parties for adults. Age and what type of party (birthday, Halloween, etc.) will help you narrow down some options. If you're doing this as a Halloween party, do you want to involve ghosts, monsters, etc.? If it is a birthday party, maybe the story line is based around spies, fairies, etc.

Age is your biggest factor in story development. In previous chapters, we discussed the learning objective targeting; now you just need to wrap a story around them. Most of my parties are hosted around Halloween, which is why the examples below are themed as such.

When you get to the example parties, you will see I do not make them scary at all, just your generic cartoon type ghosts, vampires etc. As the kids get older you can change this of course. I did so for the first time using the clown-based storyline shown last in the examples. They were not scared at all, so it might be time to ramp it up…

It would be simple enough to create a game around a fairy tale, favorite movie, favorite animal, animals in general, even a song. Search for story ideas using the internet. Heck, if you look up 'kids party ideas', you will get tons of subject matter and ideas to build off of.

I also like to take advantage of something going on at my house - construction of a shed or garage, for example. Also, any topics the kids would be talking about at school (clowns, Bloody Mary, Slender Man, etc.) or even things talked about in science class. I used all this to help build my story baseline.

As discussed in the adult version of this book, check into any local legends. These can range from hidden gold from the Civil War to money hidden and never found from a bank robbery. Maybe this gold or money is suspected to be on your property. The players could find the money, clues to who stole it, etc.

Checking into the local history of your area can easily become an educational experience. Learn about the Indians or other inhabitants that previously lived there, history of the street names, architectural styles of the houses, geology, etc.

Ask the longtime residents in the neighborhood about the area. Do they know of any mysteries, odd happenings, etc.? You never know what you will turn up that can be used to learn more about the area and be included in your mystery party.

Another option is to include some classic literature, cartoons, etc. This can be another opportunity to pick up on what the kids might be reading at school, are interested in, or just to introduce them to something new. In the adult book, I referenced Nancy Drew mysteries and even Scooby Doo to help generate ideas. The same ideas apply here with the kid's parties.

Difference Between Puzzles and Clues

I spend a little more time discussing the difference between puzzles and clues in the adult party's book, but I will summarize it here. Knowing the difference will help you in your game design, set up, and execution.

Question: What is the difference between a puzzle and a clue?
Answer: A clue is an item that is needed to solve the mystery and a puzzle is what needs to be solved to obtain that clue. For the kid's parties this might be one in the same, depending on the age and complexity level of the game.

Question: Do all clues need to be puzzles?
Answer: No, some clues can simply be found, read out of a book (which is used as a prop for the game), given at a certain time, etc. As a matter of fact, there should be more clues than puzzles to make the game move along and for people to not get stuck with nothing happening in the game.

Once you have a solid story line, you can pull out key facts or achievements needed, and use these as the clues that need to be found to solve the mystery. Some of these clues can be turned into puzzles that must be solved in order to obtain the clue. Typically you will want to make the most important facts or objectives (what drives the story), the most difficult to obtain or figure out. Making them into puzzles is a way to accomplish this. For the kid's parties, you can split larger tasks into much smaller, more easily achievable, items and goals.

I have included the same diagram I use for the adult parties (see fig. 1). This is a visual representation of the relationship between puzzles and clues. Notice the thicker line on the left, labeled story line, has a "Beginning" and an "End". Imagine this to be your story line. Now imagine taking out pieces of your story line, making the line discontinuous. You could never reach the end of the line with those pieces missing. Each of those pieces is a clue, and when the clues are placed back into the story line, you can reach the end. So as stated before, the clues can simply be important pieces of the story line: a time, place, name, letter, number, etc. An adult party should contain many more clues and puzzles than what is represented in the figure. For a children's party, particularly for young ones, this might not be too far off from an actual scenario.

For each of the removed pieces of the story line, which are considered clues, you can decide how the players will obtain the clue. On the diagram I have added, 'placed' and 'puzzle'. A placed clue is simply the clue hidden someplace. It is the actual time, place, name, letter, number, etc. that is missing from the story line. These are easy clues, since once found they reveal a part of the story line. The other type I have is a puzzle. These are puzzles that need to be solved before the clue can be revealed. Your clues or puzzles can be generated from the learning guidelines and objects.

For more complex situations, I have also indicated a double puzzle. This is a situation where a puzzle must be solved to reveal a clue. This clue in turn is needed to reveal the clue missing from the story line. For example, the players must first decode a number/letter key, which reveals the combination to a locked box which contains the last will and testament of Dr. Frankenstein. As you can see from the diagram, once you have your story line created, you simply need to pull out key facts and figure out how your players are going to go about obtaining them.

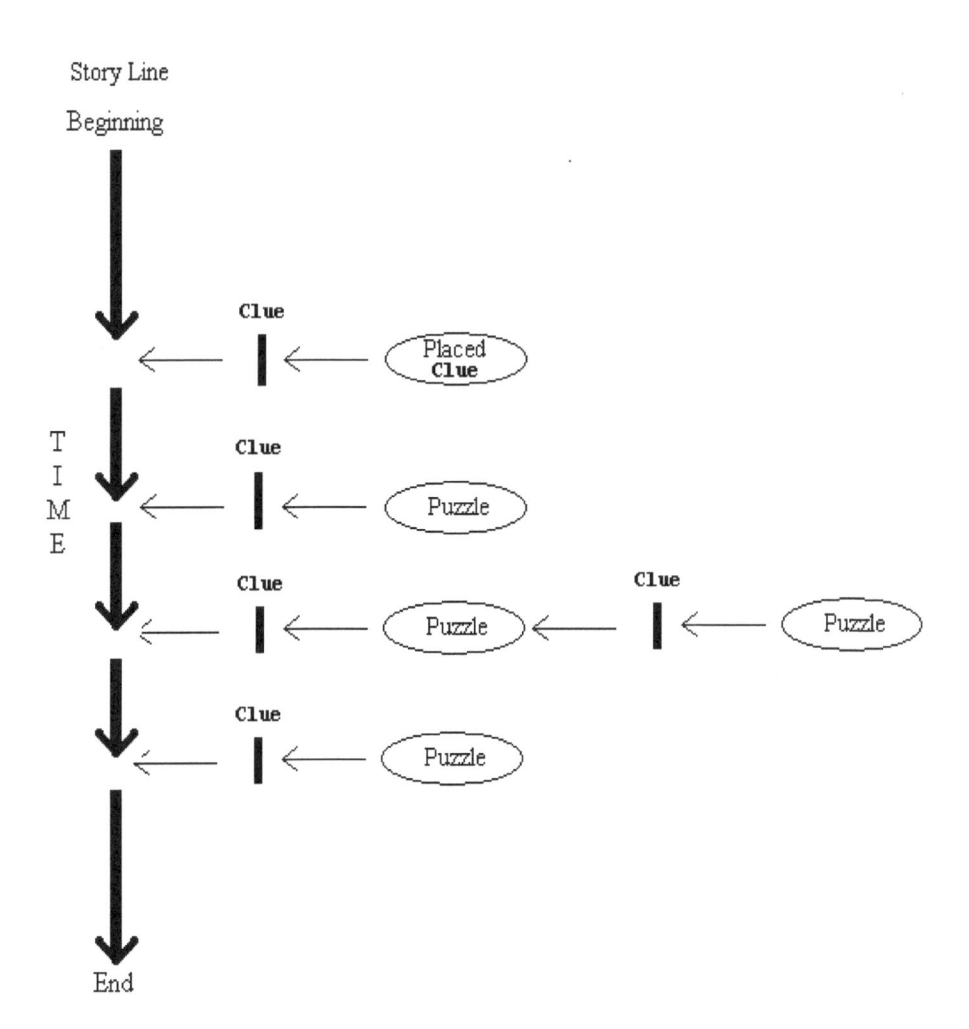

Fig. 1

Game Set Up

The initial game set up premise will vary from party to party, but the general procedure is the same.

The first thing to consider is your story line. With children and their imaginations, this can be endless. Along with a story line, you should have objectives you want the players to achieve during the game, particularly if you are trying to target specific items in the learning objectives.

The nice thing with children's imaginations is their flexibility, so your initial story line can just be a basic idea. You can build upon this idea, particularly since a number of details and new variations will come to you during creation and even during the actual set up of the game. Keep in mind you are creating a mystery/adventure party for children, so you want the basic plot to be flexible as to give you room to add in clues and puzzles depending on number of kids and age level.

You also want to keep it fun, active, and physical. Most kids are not going to want to sit for long periods of time trying to figure out a heavy logic puzzle. Know your players and custom tailor the game, puzzles, and clues to their likes, skill sets, and activity level.

The first example in this book was designed for kids under the age of 5. The game has a very simple premise: "A Halloween ghost has left clues on how to find a hidden treasure. The clues can be found all around the yard and will help you find a puzzle to solve. If you do not find the treasure in time, it will disappear!"

At this party we had a mix of ages, the oldest being 5. I designed the party so younger kids would find clues and the older kids would begin trying to solve the main puzzle using those clues. At some parties I would color code clues. Blue was for kids 5 and under, Red was for kids 6 and older. This keeps everyone busy and challenged. Most of the time it was simply a large blue or red dot on the clue.

Props, clues, puzzles, etc. can be as simple as paper print-outs or as intricate as fully constructed items. For the initial party in this book, most items were just print-outs, with the larger puzzles printed on poster size paper for all to view. Use what resources you have available and custom tailor the party to that.

As I mentioned in my first book, there are no limits to how your imagination can expand on custom tailoring your party. Your hobbies, your guest's hobbies/interests, etc., all of these can become part of the story. Maybe the victim's soul was put inside your dog, cat, or iguana - now they can be a part of the party too!

Game Play & Design

With any mystery party, you can have physical clues, riddles, math puzzles, word puzzles, etc. all based on the learning objectives or just plain fun. This is also one of the places where you can control how hard the game is, and also how many clues you need to have depending on the size of your party. Remember kids need to be entertained when they are being challenged. If during one of my kid's parties, the kids are quiet, something has gone wrong. They are usually running around looking for clues, laughing, and even sometimes arguing over any given situation. It is always very active to the point where you might ask yourself, why did I volunteer to do this?? Just keep in mind that the kids will all have fun and learn something.

With some of my past parties, I was convinced that the kids thought it was boring or not any fun. In the end, I have never had a kid or parent relay that situation to me, it has always been quite the opposite.

Another way to design a party is through 'reverse engineering'. That is to say, I have a list of learning objectives I want them to achieve, experiments I want to demonstrate, etc. From that point I would build a party around those objectives.

With the adult murder mystery parties I have done, for the most part, one of the guests at the party was the antagonist, i.e. an actual human. For the children's mystery parties the antagonist is usually imaginary – ghosts, wizards spells, hidden treasure, dolls, etc. Obviously this avoids any one child being singled out, possibly picked on, etc. This does not mean it cannot be done, I just have not incorporated that yet. As the kids get older, I am sure I will have a few that do not mind being the 'bad guy'.

Since the antagonist is not present, you will need to decide how the mystery is solved. Do they need to find a location, an item, release a trapped ghost, etc.? In the examples below, you will find each of these to use directly or as a baseline.

During the creation of your party, you will need to decide on the approximate number of clues available to the players. This is based on how many children will be in attendance as well as how difficult you want the game to be.

How to actually reveal these clues to your players is also something else to take into account. For the initial children's parties, especially the younger ones, I started with the very simple paper type clues. Most of these where 'hidden' or just scattered around the yard, making it a fast paced, run around and collect clues type of party.

One technique I have used a number of times, very successfully, is to separate clues by height. For kids under five, the clues and hints were at ground level or maybe up to 2 feet (bushes, pots, etc.) above ground. Older kids were told not to collect any clue that was below their waist height. For the older kids, I could hide clues in hard-to-find places, and even require them to climb (trees, ladders, walls, etc.). This kept everyone busy.

As the kids age, it is easy enough to make this technique harder, simply by hiding the clues better.

For the adult murder mystery parties, special care must be taken to close any loose ends that start to develop. The nice thing about the kid's mysteries, is most loose/open ends can be easily 'repaired' on the fly. You can prepare by running through the whole party at least three times on your own or if you have someone that is not going to play, have them help find potential problems. You basically need to solve all your puzzles with matching clues, looking for loopholes (kids love finding these), to minimize any problems. This will help to ensure that you have all your puzzles, clues, props, etc. leading in the right 'direction' for your solution and any other reveals or relevant events. After doing this a while, most of the time I can run through it all in my head, unless there are some mechanisms involved that need to be tested. If (more like when …) a situation arises where you have forgotten or overlooked a scenario, kids are pretty forgiving. Kids have open minds and imagination, and you can typically patch things up pretty quickly. Just keep it fun and all will be forgiven.

In preparation for the party, start writing down what props you may need to buy or create, such as maps, diaries, treasure chests, etc.

Clarify anything about how the game works and the do's and don'ts. With children, pay special attention to any safety issues and places that are off-limits during the game. Get some of the yellow caution tape if need be. You would be surprised at how quickly a child can get displaced during a game. Especially when it becomes hectic with kids running around looking for clues. Possibly have some parents help out to keep things under control so you don't find a kid looking through your underwear drawer for clues!

Go over with the kids how to win, if you play with a win option. I typically have a rule sheet that I write up and pass out. Examples of these are included in each of the sample games where they apply. Also give the players any starting clues or story lines they will need to get them going. I typically call all the kids together and do a quick story that explains the situation, what needs to be done, and any of the rules they need to follow. Sometimes the kids will have questions right off the bat.

Game Help

    Incorporation of a 'Game Help' system is especially important with children's games; the younger they are the more help they will need and the more help you should give to keep things moving and fun.

    Game help with younger kids can be as simple as observing game play and giving hints directly when needed. This was how I worked it with the younger kids. I also had some of the parents there and explained to them what type of help they are allowed to give. The whole idea is to keep the game moving and avoid the kids getting upset or bored because they are stuck. Again, we are in this for fun and sneaking in some education. Mill about as the kids are playing and simply offer some hints where you feel it is needed.

    When the kids get a little older, the help system I describe below is similar to the help system I use for the adult games. The help system of a game can serve two purposes:

1) To actually help players.
2) To add another time control factor.

    Game help can speed up or slow down the pace of the game. This is great for preventing lulls, especially important with younger kids, as mentioned. I also really suggest you integrate some kind of timing technique during the game. My usual help system is done by dispensing 'help' tickets. I use a role of red raffle type tickets, but at some point, I will make official help tickets. As I walk around watching over the party, I drop tickets on the floor, or I just hide them as I would clues.

    The ticket entitles the finder to ask me one question about the mystery, which I answer, at my discretion of course. With the children's parties I am much more generous with information. Adult parties it is limited to non-pivotal yes/no questions.

    Using this system is a great way to help move a game along. If your players are having a tough time or are not making progress, start dropping more question tickets or simply give away some information.

    During your opening discussion with your players, let them know about the help system and tickets. Your players will then know what to look out for and how to use them. When a player approaches me with a question, I will bring them to the side to avoid any other players from listening in. If the game seems to be stalled or something I perceived as easy has become seemingly hard, I will announce a hint for all to hear.

Some other options to move a stalled game forward: each child can ask five (or as many as you wish) questions, children can ask a question every 10 or 20 minutes, tell me one fact and you get two in return, etc.

Timing

The timing of your game is important, particularly with children. Timing will determine a number of factors, including how long the game is supposed to last, how long you make it actually last, and how much fun your players are having.

Timing techniques for children's games are the same for adult games, with everything just happening faster.

One simple technique to control the timing of a game is to limit the amount of clues the players can find at any given time. For example, let's say you have a total of fifty clues that need to be found to solve the entire mystery. Don't put out all fifty clues right away, as this might lead to the game ending much faster than planned. This can also cause a lot of confusion. Pacing the course/progress of the game, using the solved riddles and clues, is the suggested approach. When one clue/riddle is solved, start putting out the next one for example. Because of this, I usually just put out a few clues and then judge how the game is going. Pacing your clues is key.

Some easy ways to control the games with clues:

- If the players are having trouble, put out more clues.
- If players are figuring things out quickly, wait a while before you put out more. Players do not know how many clues there are and will keep looking for more.
- If you're using paper clues, tear some in-half to double them.

Puzzle difficulty is another game timing technique. The harder the puzzles are, the longer it will take them to solve. This can also be controlled using the help system you incorporate if things get too hard. Pay particular attention with the kids' games and the game being stalled. Kids will get bored very fast and just begin to wander or just start on something else not related to the game, for example, digging up your garden, starting a game of hide a seek, bare knuckle boxing, etc.

In an emergency situation you might need to think on your feet. If your game is supposed to last 30 minutes (a good time for the younger kids), but your players have been able to solve some major puzzles in 5 minutes and you only have five more clues to put out and no more puzzles to solve, this is a bad situation. Since you can't go back in time, your game is going to be shorter than planned. But, since you have five clues left, see if you can half or even triple those clues somehow. If they are paper clues, just rip them in half, as mentioned above. Be reasonable with this, don't make it too obvious and make sure you still keep the game moving.

One technique that I use to my advantage is general party games. Since we have most of the mysteries during our annual Halloween parties, we always have additional party games, such as apple bobbing, a piñata, pumpkin bowling, etc. I use these games to my advantage in a few ways. While the kids are playing the games, it gives me time to put out more clues, set additional things up, evaluate how things are going, etc. It also gives the kids (and me!) a break and another activity for them to enjoy. Sometimes I will even hide clues in the piñata or someplace else if the party game allows. You probably won't be able to run the party games as well. Have someone else be in charge of the party games in order to free you up.

Another aspect you need to consider is how long to run a game. This varies a lot depending on the age of the kids playing. With really young kids, the maximum time I would design the game for was 30 minutes, with kids around the age of ten, 60 minutes is max. This is never exact and also depends on a number of factors, number of kids, location, weather, amount of additional activities, etc.

The game can of course run as long as you wish. The thought has crossed my mind to have a weekend sleepover party. Letting the game span over the course of two days can lead to a number of other fun possibilities for the kids and even adults. How can I resist the temptation of a midnight haunting (scare the heck out of the kids!) over a Halloween sleepover?

Keeping Kids Involved

    The main goal for your party should be for the kids to have fun, hopefully exercise their brains, and learn something as well. It will be pretty obvious if the kids are not having a good time. I will mention again, the last party I had, I was almost positive the kids were not having a good time. There was not much laughing, smiling, excitement, etc. When I spoke to the kids afterwards, it turned out they were just really focused on the puzzles and they loved it.

    Watch for kids grouping together and making things secretive. When I have mixed ages, I strive to set the game up so that they must work together to solve the puzzles. As mentioned previously, having certain clues and puzzles only accessible to certain age groups makes them work together for a common goal.

    During one party, we had only one really young child. He was a little shy and did not know most of the other kids. I decided to make him the 'holder of hints'. As the party would move along, I would feed him some hints. The other kids had to come over to talk with him. He quickly realized the power he was wielding and was strutting around like a peacock, very proud of himself. It was fun to watch the transformation and to have him now pretty much the center of attention.

    If need be, I will bend the rules slightly to help kids out, remember fun is the objective.

    Another technique that can be used, especially when you know ahead of time which children are coming to the party, is specialty puzzles and/or clues. If children at the party have special talents or abilities, use them to your advantage, particularly if the child is shy or new to the group. For example, you have a child that can speak a foreign language, can juggle, do a backflip, etc., try to incorporate that into the story so they have a singular role in helping to solve the mystery. This is fun to do and really personalizes the game for the kids and makes them feel like they are an important part to solving the mystery. Before the party you can ask parents if their children have any special talents; this will be a huge help in preparation.

Game Ending

There are lots of options for game ending scenarios with the kids parties. I will always verify that they have solved the mystery or gotten to the main objective. I definitely go over the puzzles and make sure all are aware of the solutions, the outcomes, and sometimes solicit what they liked and disliked. It really depends on the kids and what is happening next at the party. I would make sure there are no unanswered questions as to what happened and how it all worked out in the end.

At some parties I have implemented an award system. I have done everything from prizes for the puzzle solvers and MVPs, to a found treasure chest of trinkets, access to dessert, etc. While all this is going on, hopefully in the end, you also have had fun and feel satisfaction in a job well done.

Advance Game Play

In my adult version of this book, the game runs a little differently. The antagonist is one of the players and they know what their job is, to be bad, give misinformation, create confusion, etc. while staying undetected. I have not incorporated this aspect into the kids' games yet, but as they become teenagers, I will give it a shot. I am going to include this section as a possible advanced game play option you can begin using when you feel your kids are ready.

To include the advanced game play option, as stated, one of guests at the party is the 'bad guy'. They know that this is their role and will be trying to protect themselves and remain undercover. The other players at the party will have no idea who the antagonist is, never mind that it could be an actual person at the party. Not getting caught is part of the antagonist's job.

I typically do not tell the antagonist who they are until the time of the party; this will avoid any slips of the tongue prior to the party. This approach also means that you must be flexible in who you pick. Don't put yourself in a corner by not being able to change the evil wizard's hair color for example. If that blonde kid you chose to be the evil wizard does not show up, the blonde hair clue you created will cause you some trouble.

The procedure I use for the adult party can be used in the kid version as well. Once all your guests have arrived, set yourself up in an area that is private, where the other guests can't hear you talking. Ask one of your guests to randomly call another guest to be the first to talk to you. At this point you explain the basic rules of the game, explaining to them that the 'Evil Wizard', for example, is another one of the guests and they know they are the 'bad guy'. Just make sure you spend the same amount of time with each person, as not to make it obvious you spent more time with one person and therefore, they must be the 'Evil Wizard'.

For most of the kids' parties this approach was not necessary. At the beginning of the party I was able to make a general announcement to everyone to get the party started. As kids get older, there will begin to be a merger of the adult style antagonist concept and the open-ended kids' games.

Halloween Ghost
Sample Game One
Ages 2-5

    This was one of my first parties and serves as a very simple example. This one is quick, and I have included everything you should need if you want you run this one unaltered. All you will need to do is create a board. I had access to a large printer, but you can always have it printed at an office store, such as Staples, or simply just draw it.

    After I gathered all the kids in a room, I told them. "A Halloween ghost has left a poster on how to find a hidden treasure. He has left clues all around the yard and you must solve the puzzle to find the treasure. If you do not find it soon, it will disappear."

    I had a mixture of ages at this one, so I had the youngest kids in charge of finding the clues and the older kids trying to decipher them.

    The poster board, shown below, is what was hanging up for all the kids to see.

    Each of the items on the board represent a word in a sentence, there are 11 words they need to figure out.

For the 11 words, I originally just had 11 paper clues that I created. If you need to make the game more challenging or you have more kids coming than originally planned, clues can simply be torn in half. This means players would first have to find the two halves, then solve the clue. Solving the clue leads to the word. For example, on one side of a paper clue it reads "2+2" on the other it reads "LOOK".
Knowing that 2+2=4, and 4 being the first in the series of the ghost sentence, the first word of the sentence is "LOOK".

Full clue sequence:

Clue 1: One side reads "2+2" the other reads "LOOK", this will match to the number 4 on the board.

Clue 2: One side reads "Meow" the other reads "FOR", this will match to the cat on the board.

Clue 3: One side reads "7 Days" the other reads "A", this will match to "1 Week" on the board.

Clue 4: One side shows a picture of 10 pennies the other reads "ROPE", this will match the dime on the board.

Clue 5: One side reads "Half Circle" the other reads "ATTACHED", this will match to semicircle on the board.

Clue 6: One side reads "1:00" the other reads "TO", this will match to clock on the board.

Clue 7: One side shows a picture of a bee, the other reads "A", this will match to a beehive on the board.

Clue 8: One side shows a picture of a Saturn rocket, the other reads "TREE", this will match to the moon on the board.

Clue 9: One side reads "Red + Yellow" the other reads "IN", this will match the orange square on the board.

Clue 10: One side shows a picture of batteries, the other reads "THE", this will match to the battery box on the board.

Clue 11: One side shows a picture of rain, the other reads "FRONT", this will match to the cloud on the board.

Fully decoded message:
"LOOK FOR A ROPE ATTACHED TO A TREE IN THE FRONT"

During this party all kids were kept in the backyard, removing the chance for the rope to be accidentally discovered. Once the clue is read, the stampede to the front of the house ensued.

The rope was fastened to the tree with the other end hanging over a branch. There was a bag attached to the other end. See simple drawing below.

I put the end attached to the tree high enough so only I could release the bag or boost a kid up to release it. Most of the time kids want to be where the bag will drop. Inside the bad was similar items you would find in a Piñata: candy, small toys, etc. Kids loved it! Obviously, the clues can be changed to anything you want the kids to find. You can add more clues for a more complex game or a larger party, etc.

Trail of the Vampire
Sample Game Two
Ages 3-6

The second game I set up for kids was actually easier than the first. I made this one a little easier since we were not going to have many older kids at the party. Because of these factors I made this primarily a seek-find game, as well as added in a dress-up portion. There also is a little trick I played on the kids by the end of the party.

For set up, I ordered a cheap cardboard-cutout Vampire online. It was just used as a visual prop which I modified. I also ordered all the items used in this mystery in bulk. These appear in the checklist below.

The main objective of the party was to track down a vampire using clues and a little history. During this process, the kids will need to find the actual items from the checklist. The funny part about this is as the kids find these items, most of the kids will start wearing them, not realizing they are turning themselves into a vampire. By the end of the party you should have a bunch of little vampires running around.

To track down the vampire, they have to find a list of items and solve one clue. Pretty easy.

I described the party and objective to the kids. Off they went, searching for each clue/item. They had the option of trying to find them all at once or one by one. In either case, they had to check in with me so I could verify they have found the items. At this time, I would also suggest that they wear it, if they had not done so already.

The non-clue items included a set of the classic vampire teeth, a black cape (actually a large plastic garbage bag that I made into a cape), a fang ring, and necklace that had some teeth on it.

The clue items were paper. The paper clues were plentiful, so every kid had a chance to find enough to solve the clues. For this party we had a lot of kids, so I tore the paper clues in half. There were 2 clues:

1. The letters V,A,M,P,I,R,E were on individual small pieces of paper.
2. The clue they would find for this was a piece of paper with "$1000 + 431 = ?$". Vlad the Impaler, possibly the basis of the story of Dracula, was born in 1431.

Kids enjoyed, and, in the end, thought it was funny that while searching for the Vampire, they 'became' one. We had fruit punch to drink as well, which of course I told them was really blood after they all drank it. The prizes were the items they found. This party was simple and not competitive between children. Each child could solve the clues on their own.

Each child was given this checklist at the beginning of the party:

Check List

☐ Vampire Teeth

☐ Cape

☐ 7 Letters of His Name

☐ Fang Ring

☐ Year He was Born

☐ Vampire Necklace

Pirates Treasure
Sample Game Three
Ages 4+

My son and daughter have birthdays that are pretty close together. They also have mutual friends. In this case we decided to combine the parties into a not so surprising scenario, Princesses (for the girls) and Pirates (for the boys). Regretfully we left the party favors unguarded and, with pirates afoot, that had disastrous consequences, as you will see below.

Set up for the party:

"A band of evil pirates has pillaged John and Jenn's birthday party and stolen all the party favors! They put all the treasure in a pirate's chest, hid the chest, locked it, and then hid the key as well!

Each of the evil pirates is hiding a piece of the treasure map and some of those pirates are hiding too. The 'good' pirates need to get all the pieces of the map, put them together and then figure out where the treasure chest is hidden.

The princesses need to find the key to the treasure chest. Butterflies are trying to help you find the key. Look for yellow butterflies and they will help lead you to the key…

'Good' pirates can help the princesses after they find the locked treasure chest.

<u>You will need to all work together as a team.</u>"

This party was a last-minute situation, so I went with the golden standard, paper puzzle clues. I was able to throw together the treasure box shown below. It was 2-foot square, so it was a nice size. I had the lock and chain laying around and I made some skull and crossbones embellishments.

For the boys' treasure map, I drew a section of my yard using Microsoft Paint. Depending on how many kids were showing up would dictate how many pieces I tore the map into. The map I used is below. To give it more of a pirate map feel and look, I burned the edges. This eventually was torn into lots of smaller pieces as kids arrived at the party. Skull and Crossbones marks the spot where the treasure box was hidden. It was behind a bunch of large bushes and could not be accessed from behind.

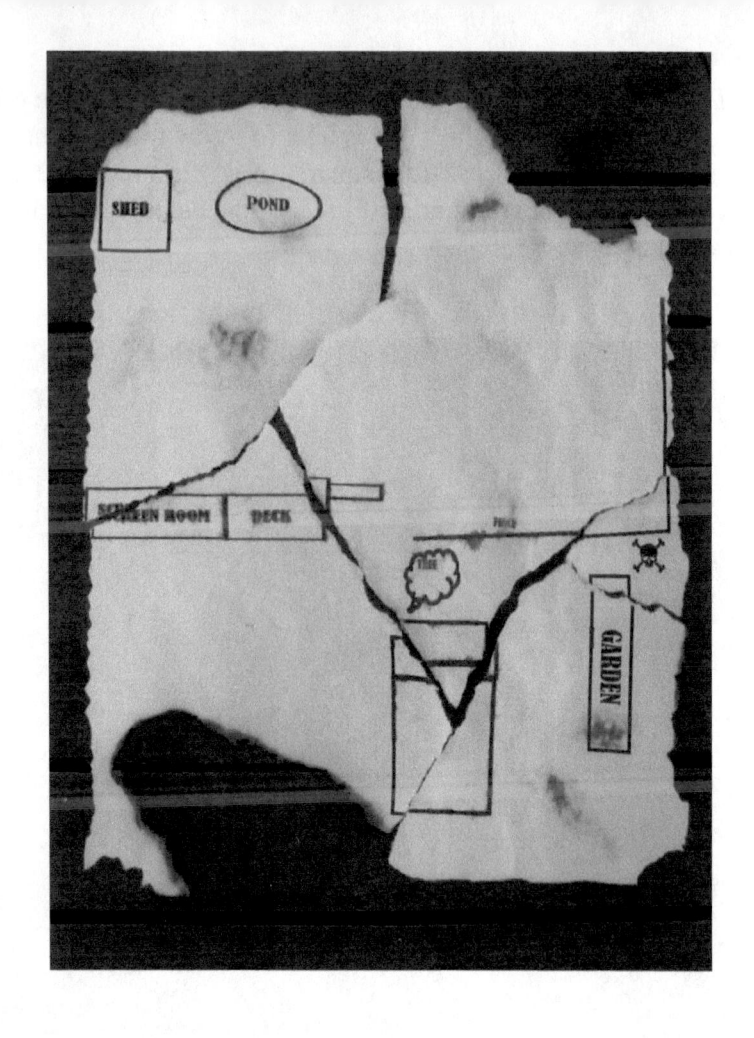

For the girls' butterflies, I printed and cut out what you see below.

On the back of each butterfly was one word. The butterflies needed to be assembled to form a sentence that reveled the location of the hidden key needed to open the treasure chest.

In this case there were 8 butterflies with a message that read:

"You will find the key under the slide"

Because of the number of kids showing up at the party, I had to cut up the butterflies to make the game more challenging. Also notice that each wing has a shape in each the corner, except for the first and last words of the sentence. These were put on to help the kids organize the words into the correct order. They had to match circle to circle, square to square, etc.

The key was hidden under a slide in our yard. Once the pirates were able to locate the treasure chest, which was well hidden behind some bushes and the princesses were able to locate the key, they dragged out the chest and opened the box to reveal lots of treasure.

Lots of treasure!

The kids really enjoy these paper jigsaw type party puzzles. They are easy to create, follow, are active, and the difficulty can be altered simply by increasing the number of clues.

Zombie Hunt
Sample Game Four
Ages 5+

    This party was a little more involved because it has an active antagonist. One of the people at the party is assigned the roll of being a zombie. I also upped the difficulty and variety of clues and questions. As always, we had a large age differential and had a lot of kids. To help manage the amount of kids, as well as make it fun and fair, I changed the clue system around a little. I decided to make only certain clues available for certain ages. This was a color-coded system explained in the party opener:

"There is a Zombie at the party and you have to figure out who it is, but keep it to yourself so you can win the game!

Clues with a Blue Dot are for kids in kindergarten or below.

Clues with a Red Dot are for kids first grade or older.

Find the clues and try to figure out who it is…

If you find the same clue or the wrong color, leave it for someone else."

    Again, pretty straight forward instructions and ways to sort the clues between kids.

    Since this book is in black & white and the dots are repetitive, I have just included the clue and a description of the dot layout used. You can add your own creativity to this portion as well as how big you want to make the dots. You will see some obvious education correlations here as well.

Blue Clues
(Kindergarten and under)

Actual blue dots have been removed for clarity

- How many dots are on this page? (There were 5 blue dots)

- What shape are the circles in? (Dots were in a triangle shape)

- What will happen if you heat up ice? (It melts)

- Give me a word that rhymes with ghost. (many answers here)

- What is inside the circle? (A witch)

- What do you plant in the ground to grow a cucumber plant? (A seed)

- How many fingers across is this line? (Kids measure line with their own fingers)

 _____

- What rhymes with witch? (Many answers here)

- How many fingers do you have? (Usually 10)

- What comes first, breakfast or lunch? (Breakfast)

- Name one thing that flies in the sky? (Bird, plane, etc.)

- What do you hear with? (Ears)

- What do you smell with? (Nose)

- How many legs does a dog have? (Usually four)

- What color is an orange? (Orange)

- What is this? (Our moon)

- What animal uses its tongue to smell? (Snake)

- Count to ten. (…)

Red Clues
(1st grade and up)

Actual red dots have been removed for clarity

- What comes next, 54, 53, 52 … (51)

- What is two dimes and a penny equal to? (21 cents)

- What is heavier a real cat or a dog? (Usually the dog)

- What comes after Thursday? (Friday)

- Is this true   12 = 6+6? (yes)

- What is this? (Flathead screwdriver)

- What does a plant need to grow? (water and sunlight)

- What star is closest to the Earth? (The Sun)

- Ant – Bat – Cat
  Which word should come next, Dog or Zoo? (Dog)

- Can a circle roll down a hill? (yes)

- Can you keep a snowball in the freezer? (yes)

- What creature has a skeleton on the outside? (insects/bugs)

- 8-4+4=? (8)

- A donut has two of what same shapes? (circles)

- What tool is this? (Pliers)

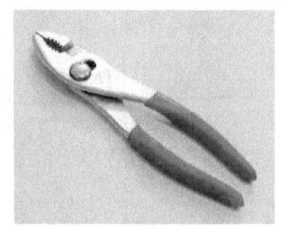

- How many inches is a foot? (12)

- How many seconds in an hour? (3600)

- When clouds fill with water, what happens? (It rains)

- 100+200-100= (200)

    Each time a player found a clue and had an answer, they could come check with me. Some of these clues were torn in half, so they had the classic paper matching component to contend with as well. If they had the correct answer to the clue, they were given another clue about who the Zombie could be.

The following are the clues:

- The zombie at this party is older than 2
- The zombie at this party is older than 4
- The zombie at this party is older than 7
- The zombie at this party is older than 10
- The zombie at this party is older than 20
- The zombie at this party is younger than 60.

- The zombie at this party is wearing pants
- The zombie at this party is wearing clothes
- The Zombie at this party has two legs
- The zombie at this party is a girl
- The zombie at this party is not a boy
- The Zombie at this party has long hair

* If you ask a zombie "Are you hungry?"
  It will answer "Yes, for you!"
  RUN!!!!!!!

Looking at the clues, you should be able to see where it was going. The zombie was one of the adults that I knew would be attending. The last clue with the asterisk is the big one, the final clue they can use to determine for sure if they have figured out who the zombie was.

After one of the kids narrows down the suspects and comes to you with a guess and you feel the party is coming to an end, let them guess. If you are not ready for the party to end, tell them there are more clues that need to be found.

When choosing your adult, pick someone who will be animated once they are outed. Have the kids gather round like an old-time witch trail to make the accusation. Have them ask the question. At the beginning of the party I let the chosen adult know they are the zombie and if asked the question "Are you hungry?" they must answer, "Yes, for you!" and them ham-it-up with a scary voice, arms in the air, etc.

Ghostly Treasure
Sample Game Five
Ages 6+

I really liked the previous party's set-up with the red and blue dots, simple clue set up and educational components. I repeated this technique for this party.

Attendance for this party were older children at "6+", as well as a large number of children that were younger.

This party was designed for 30 kids maximum; Blue Dots are for kids 5 and under, Red Dots are for kids 6 and over.

Party introduction as it was actually printed:

GHOSTLY TREASURE

LAST NIGHT I HEARD A SPOOKY NOISE! WHEN I WENT TO SEE WHAT IT WAS, I SAW A BABY GHOST LEAVING CLUES ALL OVER. WHEN HE SAW ME, HE SAID HE WAS HIDING A TREASURE WITH CLUES TO FIND IT ... THEN DISAPPEARED! BEFORE HE LEFT HE GAVE ME A MAP TO HELP YOU FIND THE CLUES. PARENTS, FEEL FREE TO AID THE YOUNGER KIDS WITH THE CLUES.

Blue Clues
(Kids 5 and under)

HOW MANY GHOSTS ARE IN THIS PICTURE?

WHAT SHAPES DO YOU SEE?

IF YOU HEAT UP ICE, WHAT DOES IT TURN INTO?

WHAT IS NEXT HOLIDAY COMING UP?

WHAT JOB DO THESE PEOPLE HAVE?

WHAT INSTRUMENT IS THIS?

SHOW ME YOUR SCARED FACE.

WHAT RHYMES WITH 'TREAT'

MAKE UP A HALLOWEEN SONG AND SING IT.

WHAT INSTRUMENT IS THIS?

Red Clues
(Kids 6 and older)

25 30 35 40 45 50??

WHICH NUMBER DOES NOT BELONG?
2 4 6 8 9 12

4 + 5 + 9 = ?

WHAT'S THE SECOND DAY OF THE WEEK?

The Student Council at Jefferson Elementary held an ice cream eating contest at the school fair.

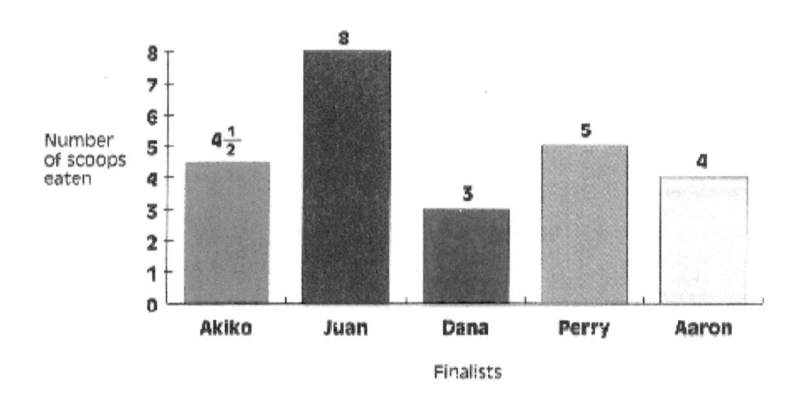

Finalist	Number of scoops eaten
Akiko	$4\frac{1}{2}$
Juan	8
Dana	3
Perry	5
Aaron	4

WHO ATE THE MOST SCOOPS?

WHICH WILL A MAGNET PICK UP?

WHERE DOES COTTON COME FROM?

IS THIS TRUE?
8 = 7

WHAT CONTINENT IS THIS?

WHAT IS A LAW?

MAKE UP A POEM ABOUT HALLOWEEN

I decided to reuse a few props I made for one of my adult parties. I will understand that most people will not be doing this, but, there are other ways to accomplish the same general idea based on your own set of skills and creativity.

For the adult party, I had created molds from plaster. The first mold I created was from a skull drinking cup I found during Halloween. I cut the cup about a quarter of the way down. I blew up a small balloon and held it in the middle of the bottom portion of the mold and pored the plaster around it, filling it to the top. The balloon created a space in the skull. I filled the top portion of the mold to make the top of the skull. I took a key (I will explain what that key is for in a minute) and sealed in the skull. This actual skull is the pictured below. If you look closely, you will notice the crack along the top, this was sealed up with more plaster after the key was placed inside.

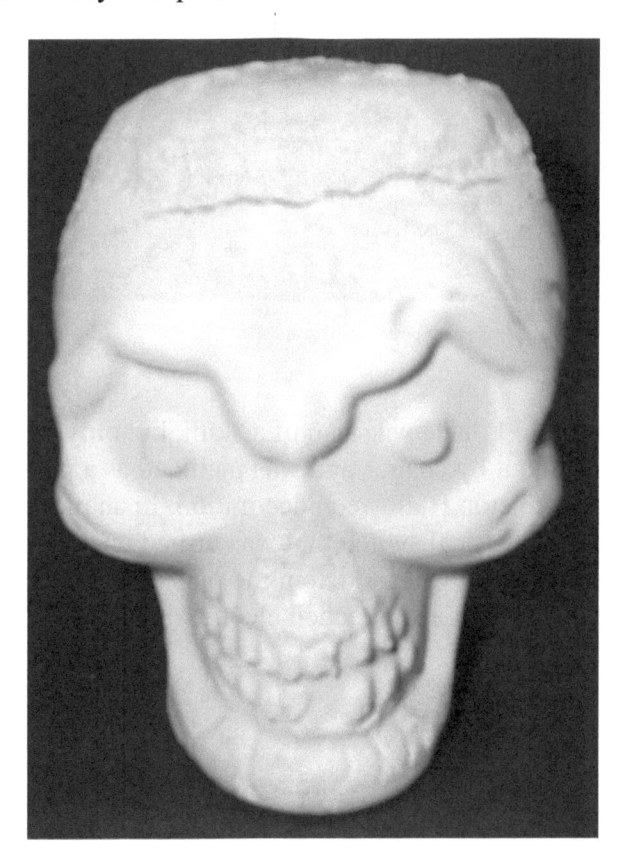

The following picture is of the open mold after I started gluing it back together for the first book. Using a C-clamp, the players were able to break it into a few pieces. I avoided making a hammer available for fear that smashing the skull would send the key flying off into the ether.

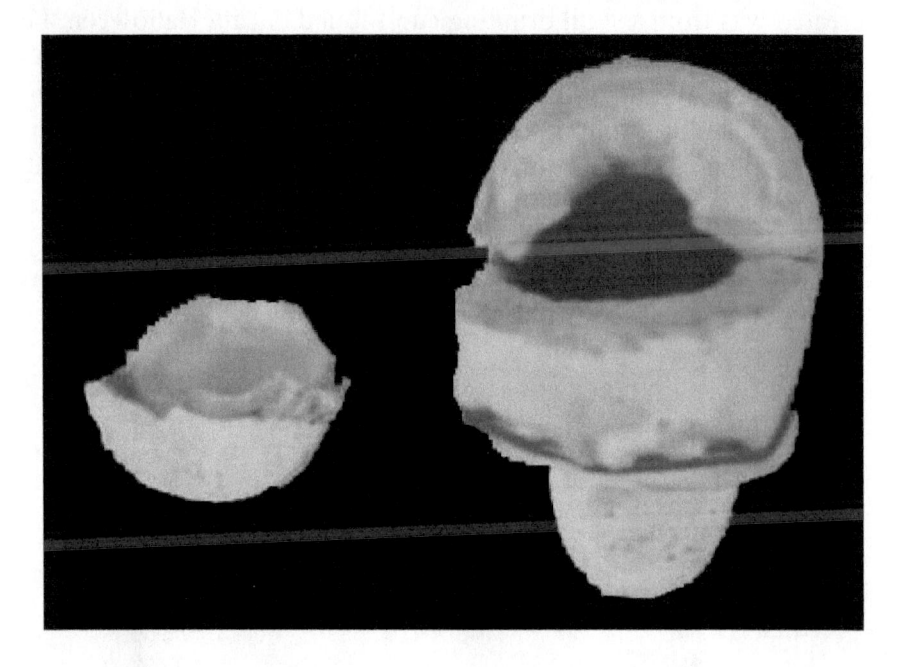

The next mold I made was also of a skull, but only of the face. This mold I came about by chance and was included as a protective cover for a singing skeleton Halloween decoration. In an old box of electrical parts, I had an electrical switch that was turned on and off with a key.

This is the key that was hidden in the plaster skull. I molded the skull around the key switch and attached electrical cords to it (see picture below).

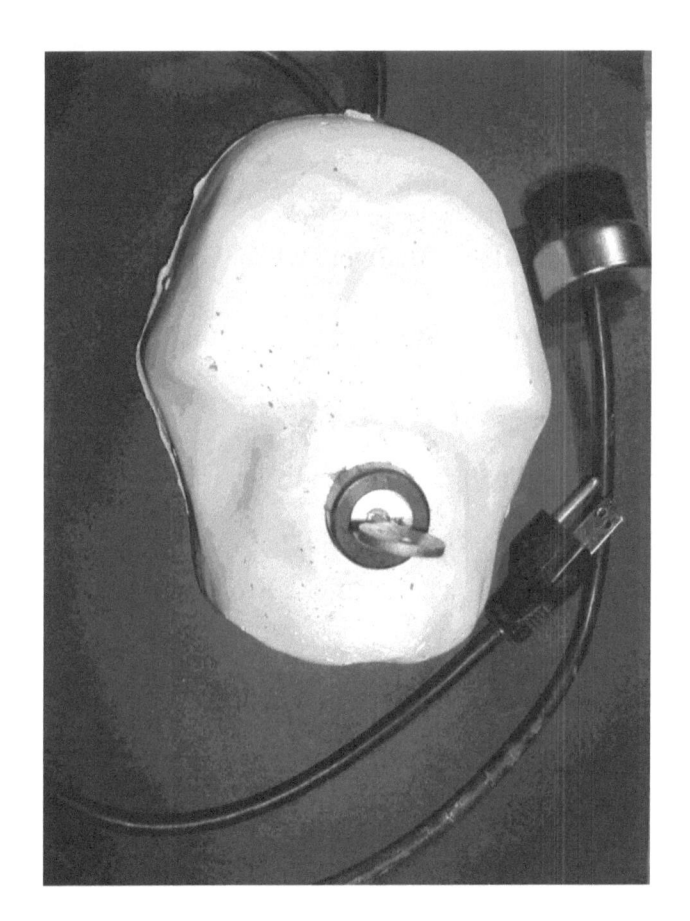

The players were trying to find clues and solve puzzles that would inevitably lead to them finding the key. As to where I decided to use this device, the fishpond in my yard seemed perfect. The fishpond has an electrical pump that drives a waterfall.
     I had a bag full of pennies (for weight) and some fake gold coins, which was tied to a long string and attached to a small balloon, the kind that comes in the water balloon kits. I disconnected the hose that ran from the pump to the waterfall and lodged the balloon in the output fixture of the pump and put it back under the water. The chain of events that occurred to enable the players to find the treasure was as follows:

1) Find all pieces of the paper clues and assemble them (Jig-Saw puzzle style) to see a diagram of skull and key inside.
3) Find hidden C-clamp.
4) Figure out, based on clues how to use C-clamp to break open skull and retrieve key.
5) Using maps and clues, figure out where skull with key switch is buried.
6) Uncover skull and use key.
7) Notice that once key is turned, pond begins churning and a balloon has surfaced.
8) Retrieve balloon and see it is attached to a string, keep pulling string until treasure is pulled from the pond.

   Once the kids have retrieved the 'gold' they could then, using their found booty, 'buy' their choice of candy or small trinket I had at the ready.

Below is the paper clue showing how to use C-clamp to break open skull to retrieve key.

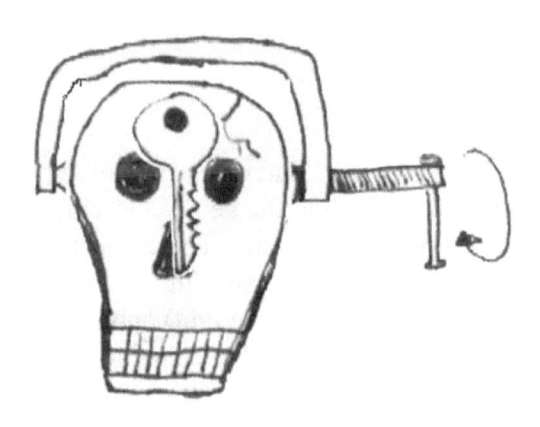

Example 'Map' of the yard that would reveal the location of key operated skull.

Haunted House
Sample Game Six
Ages 7+

If it's not broke, don't fix it. Some color-coded clues once again for this Haunted House style game. Difference is the game has a much more involved solution and deeper game play. The players need to find and solve clues, solve puzzles, find props and maps, set up ceremonial items, mix a potion, and chant a spell. Lots to do!

For this party's set up, I read what you see below out loud to the kids. I also printed it out on a large poster board. This gave them access to it for the game entirety in case they needed a review. You can do similar or just give them their own copy:

There is a rumor that this house is haunted. At night strange noises can be heard coming from whatever floor you're NOT on. Sometimes a bang, sometimes what sounds like little footsteps. Other times if you're real quiet, you can hear a voice. "Heeeeelllp Meeeeee" the voice says. If you try to follow the voice, it always sounds like it is coming from the back door of the house. If you open the back door and listen closer, it sounds like it is echoing from the whole yard. "Heeeeelp Meeee Leeeeavvve Thisssss Place"

Blue Dots are for kids 7 and under.
Red Dots are for kids 8 and over.

If your team finds a double, please give it to the other team.

Look around the yard for clues and figure out what is going on.

This party required a lot of props. Some of the props also needed to be placed in specific places in the yard. Obviously if you're trying to emulate this party, you will need to custom-tailor each of the locations.

Props and Locations

Blood (preferably fake)
Large paint brush
Scissors
Bowl to mix ingredients
Skull (any size)
Flower (fake or real)
Rock (any size)
Stick (branch from a tree)
Gate
Fence (next to the gate listed above)
Hair (small piece from a donor (explained later))
* Smoke machine (optional)

On the following pages you will find the 'blue' and 'red' clues. The answers to the clues will correspond to the items and locations above.

Red Clues
(8 and over)

1 = Igneous, Sedimentary and Metamorphic are all types of:
- Rock
- Plants
- Bugs
- Leaves

3 = The Human body has 1.2 to 1.5 gallons of this:
- Water
- Skin
- Blood
- Poop

5 = If you get a strike or a spare you are doing what? Now remove the 'ing'

7 = Nasal, Temporal, Maxilla and Mandible are all parts of the:
- Stomach
- Arm
- Skull
- Foot

9 = A freestanding structure designed to restrict or prevent movement across a boundary is a:
- Wire
- Fence
- Hole
- Stream

11 = A hinged barrier used to close an opening in a wall or fence is a:
- Gate
- Net
- Sand
- Trap Door

Blue Clues
(7 and under)

2 = These fall off the trees when it's windy, its rhymes with bricks

4 = People can have Red, Brown, Black or Blonde of this:
- Eyes
- Teeth
- Hair
- Nose

6 = When you combine or put together two or more things to form one substance or mass, you:
- Add
- Pour
- Eat
- Mix

8 = Lily, Rose and Tulip are all types of:
- Books
- Cars
- Trees
- Flowers

10 = A pair of posts linked by a crossbar and often with a net attached behind it, forming a space into or over which the ball has to be sent in order to score is a:
- Wall
- Lake
- Goal
- Soccer

The answers to the above questions lead to the prop or item the players need to use or collect.

1 = Rock
2 = Stick
3 = Blood
4 = Hair
5 = Bowl
6 = Mix
7 = Skull
8 = Flower
9 = Fence
10 = Goal
11 = Gate

The additional paper clues were a fake article I made to build the story, two additional notes from the ghost, a diagram showing the ceremonial set up, a diagram showing how to mix the potion, and, finally, the chant. The chant clue is not able to be found until most of the items have been found. Do not put it out too early.

Below is the fake article I created using a program online. I blurred my address, you will use the address of the house where the party is taking place:

The Washin

Friday, March 13, 1932

Ghost at ▬ Beach ▬ Dri

By Doug Jones

During a recent visit to ▬ Beach ▬ Drive, we discussed with the owners all the strange happenings at the house. Sounds, voices, things moving on their own. It all seems to be emanating from the yard. Lom Grund, the current owner believes there is an ancient spirit confined to the yard for some reason and it needs help leaving. Lom has found clues and hints around the yard but has never been successful in getting the ghost to leave.

We just think he is crazy!

These fake articles can also be used as the party invitation, it sets the suspense and is a fun way to introduce the party.

Additional Paper Clues

I HAVE BEEN TRAPPED HERE FOR 100 YEARS AND I NEED YOUR HELP TO ESCAPE. FOLLOW THE CLUES I HAVE LEFT. HELP!

ONCE '11' IS SET UP, SAY THE CHANT AND YOU WILL SEE ME GO IN A PUFF OF SMOKE!

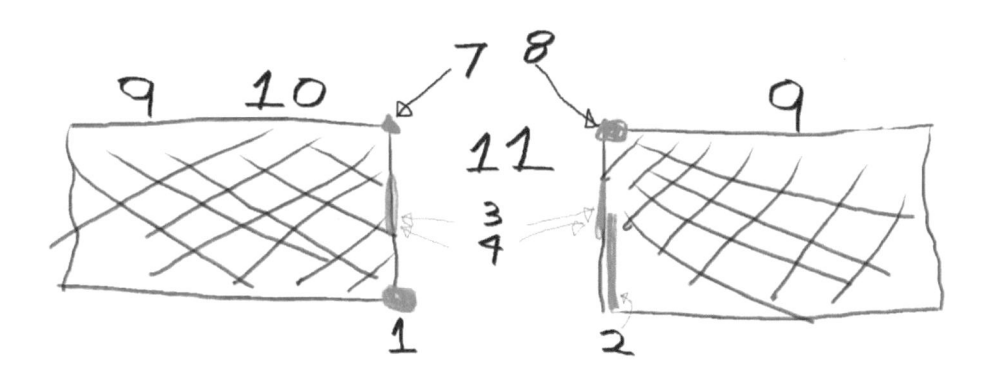

Above clue shows all the locations of where the items found must be placed. My drawings were done quickly in Microsoft Paint. If I had the time, I would have made a much more detailed drawing or taken a photo of the locations and edited the locations on the photo. 9 is the fence, 7 is the skull, etc.

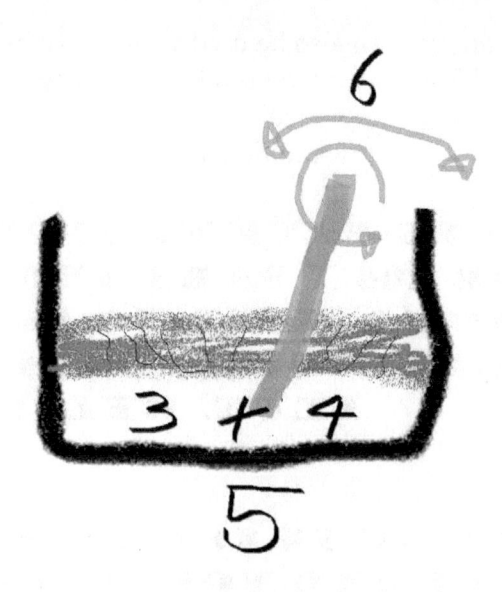

Above clue shows how the potion must be mixed with the corresponding parts and materials from the decoded clues. 3 is the 'blood', 4 is the hair, etc. The hair can be from any of the players. Once this clue comes out, you might need to do a little prompting for the players to understand someone must sacrifice a piece of their hair. Obviously this is just a tiny snip, but the kids usually make a big deal about it.

     Once the players have completed all the required steps to set up the ceremony, have them all gather together. I had multiple copies of the chant to give to the kids so they can say the chant nice and loud all together. A bunch of kids yelling this chant all together is something your neighbors will find comical or disturbing. Once the kids got to the last "NOW!!!!!!!!!!!!!", I had a smoke machine hidden in bushes right near the gate that I was able to turn on remotely. This is one of the reasons I chose the location, so I could hide the smoke machine. In a puff of smoke, the ghost is freed. On the following page is the chant I created.

<u>I hear you crying
I hear you wailing.</u>

<u>Your time has come
We set your ghost sailing</u>

<u>Out of this yard; and into nevermore
May your ghost port on any shore.
We have completed your list
Leave us in mist</u>

<u>NOW!!!!!!!!!!!!!!!!!!
I hear you wailing.
I hear you crying</u>

<u>Your time has come
We set your ghost sailing</u>

<u>Out of this yard; and into nevermore
May your ghost port on any shore.
We have completed your list
Leave us in mist</u>

<u>NOW!!!!!!!!!!!!!!!!!!</u>

Witches & Warlocks
Sample Game Seven
Ages 8+

In the previous party, I noticed the kids got really excited about mixing up that very simple 'potion'. The mixed potion really did not do anything once mixed, but the anticipation that it actually might gave me the idea here. For this party the kids will get to mix a bunch of 'potions' that actually have chemical reactions. This one gets messy!

For the verbal party set up, I gathered the kids around to set up the scenario and explain what they are going to be doing. I also added some things about safety. To help set the stage, I had on a wizards costume to play the part of the 'teacher'. You can expand on the opening, but the general premise is that today the players are Witches or Warlocks. It is their first day of training. Hidden around the yard are riddles and potion recipes. Solve a riddle and get an ingredient from the Apothecary.

Once the players had all the ingredients and a recipe they wanted to try, I had a small table set up to try the potion. They were supposed to predict what would happen. Each time, I would gather all the kids around and let them do most of the potions/experiment on their own. I had lots of supplies to let each kid give it a try. After each experiment we would talk about the results and why it happens from a scientific standpoint.

The riddles were placed out, in multiple pieces that had to be put together, as well as the answers. In some cases the kids were able to answer the riddles without needing to find the actual paper answer.

Riddles:

1. Why did the witch walk across the road?

- Because her broomstick was broken.

2. What is a Warlock's best subject in school?

- Spelling, of course.

3. What do you call two witches living together?

- Broom-mates.

4. What do witches ask for when they are in a hotel?

- Broom-service.

5. What do you call a witch who lives at the beach?

- A sand-wich.

6. Why did the Warlock cancel the baseball game?

- Because they lost their bats.

7. How do witches tell time?

- With a witch watch.

8. Why did the warlocks mail rattle?

- Because it was a chain letter.

12. How does a witch fix her hair?

- She uses scare-spray.

16. Why don't witches like to fly their brooms when they're angry?

- Because they're afraid of flying off the handle.

17. Who was the most famous witch detective?

- Warlock Holmes (Sherlock Holmes).

Potions and Chemistry

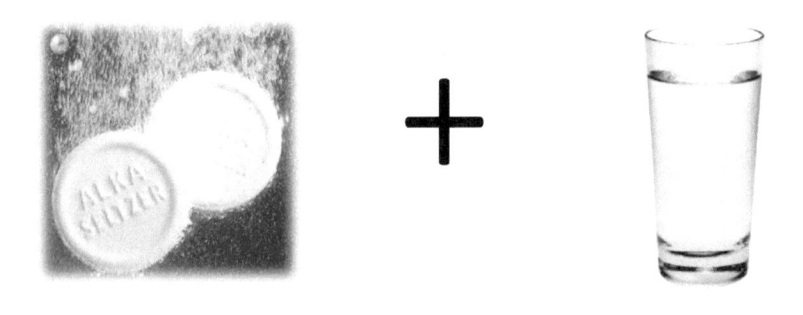

H_2O_2 = Hydrogen Peroxide

$H_3C-CO-CH_3$ = Acetone

$H_3C \overset{\overset{O}{\|}}{} CH_3$ + [cup]

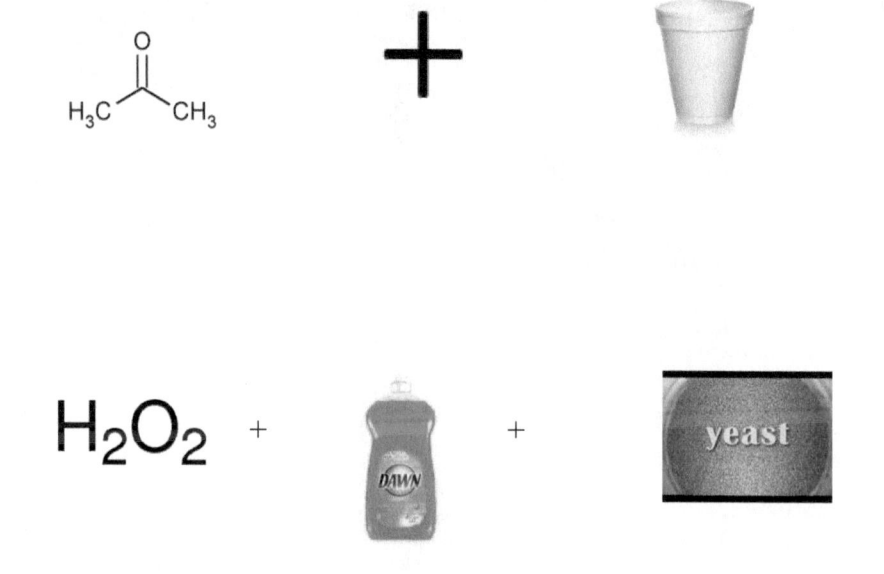

H_2O_2 + [Dawn] + yeast

- The Mentos and diet soda will cause the soda to shoot out of the top of the bottle.

- The vinegar and baking soda were put into a small sealable snack bag and thrown, eventually it will pop open or burst.

- Alka seltzer and water simply caused fizzy water they could taste.

- I helped the kids with the experiment with the acetone, as I did not want them getting the acetone on their skin or anywhere else. I let them drop/place the cup into a tray that had about a ½ inch of acetone. The cup will dissolve where it touches the acetone.

- The Hydrogen Peroxide, dish soap, and yeast will yield 'elephant toothpaste'. I would suggest looking this one up so you can decide how much of a mess you want …

- I also did another experiment, but did not offer any clues. I would ask kids who were finishing up, "If I put water in this can, heat it up, and then put it in cold water, what will happen?" Since this one used heat, I was using a propane torch. This was a demonstration showing that when a small amount of water is heated inside the can, steam is produced, filling the can. When the can is inverted into cold water, all of the steam condenses quickly causing the can to implode. Most kids were pretty impressed with my 'magic'.

   This party was a great success. The kids were very excited to get to do the experiments. The 'exploding' sealed bags were a huge hit and were done multiple times by each kid. It can definitely get out of hand with the kids all wanting to do various experiments and it definitely gets messy. I did one of the large examples of 'elephant toothpaste', but well worth it. Kids had fun and learned some basic chemistry.

Who or What?
Sample Game Eight
Ages 9+

This party was done the year clown sightings and clown stories were big in the media. Creepy clowns were being spotted in cities and towns, kids were coming home with friends-of-friend's stories about creepy clown interactions, etc. So why not jump on the band wagon? Kids did not know it was a clown-based party until he emerged from the pond!

It also helped that at the time, we were having a garage built, so I incorporated that into the story.

Party opening speech to kids, the more dramatic the better:

"WITH ALL THE CONSTRUCTION GOING ON AT OUR HOUSE, SOMETHING WAS DISTURBED DURING THE DIGGING.

CONSTRUCTION WORKERS SAID THEY WERE FINDING WEIRD THINGS BURIED IN THE GROUND. A LOT OF THESE ITEMS CAN BE FOUND AROUND THE YARD. SOMETIMES WHILE THEY WERE DIGGING, THEY WOULD HEAR STRANGE LAUGHING.

AT NIGHT, SOME OF OUR NEIGHBORS CLAIM TO HAVE HEARD WEIRD SOUNDS AND ALSO THE STRANGE LAUGHING.

VERY EARLY ONE MORNING A NEIGHBOR SAID SHE SAW SOMETHING CRAWLING INTO OUR POND. SHE COULD NOT MAKE OUT WHAT IT WAS, BUT HEARD SOME STRANGE LAUGHING.

WHAT OR WHO COULD IT BE?

LOOK AROUND FOR THE CLUES THAT WERE DUG UP, MAYBE YOU CAN HELP FIGURE IT OUT?

POND IS OFF LIMITS UNTIL YOU THINK YOU KNOW WHAT IS GOING ON AND NEED TO CHECK WITH ME FIRST."

This is the set of paper clues that were distributed around the yard, some torn in half based on the number of kids attending. They had to match those and then get all the clues in order to begin to banish the evil clown!

1/8 - I have buried him here hopefully forever.
2/8 - If he escapes he will hide until he can grow.
3/8- Look for evidence of where he might be hiding.
4/8 - If he escapes, he must be banished again to ground or sky using a banishing spell.
5/8 - The spell must be read aloud where he is hiding.
6/8 – He will try to distract you with puzzles and tricks.
7/8 - Solve his riddles fast to assemble the spell.
8/8 – Hurry, if darkness falls, he will grow …

The following were the next set of various riddles and clues that the players had to solve to receive parts to create the banishing spell.

What did the little clown do when he learned that he was going to die?
- He went into the living room.

Why did the little clown drive his car into a tree?
- He wanted to hear its bark.

How Many Triangles?
- 13

10 triangles you can count inside and outside triangle and:
- upper 3 dark triangles make a triangle
- three triangles to lower left makes a triangle
- three triangles to lower right makes a 13th triangle

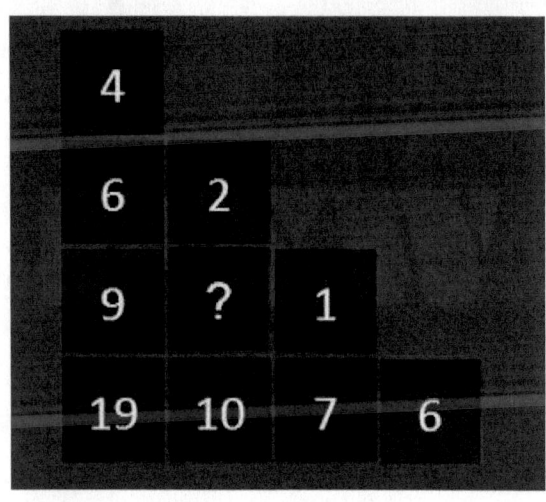

What Is The Missing Number?
- 3

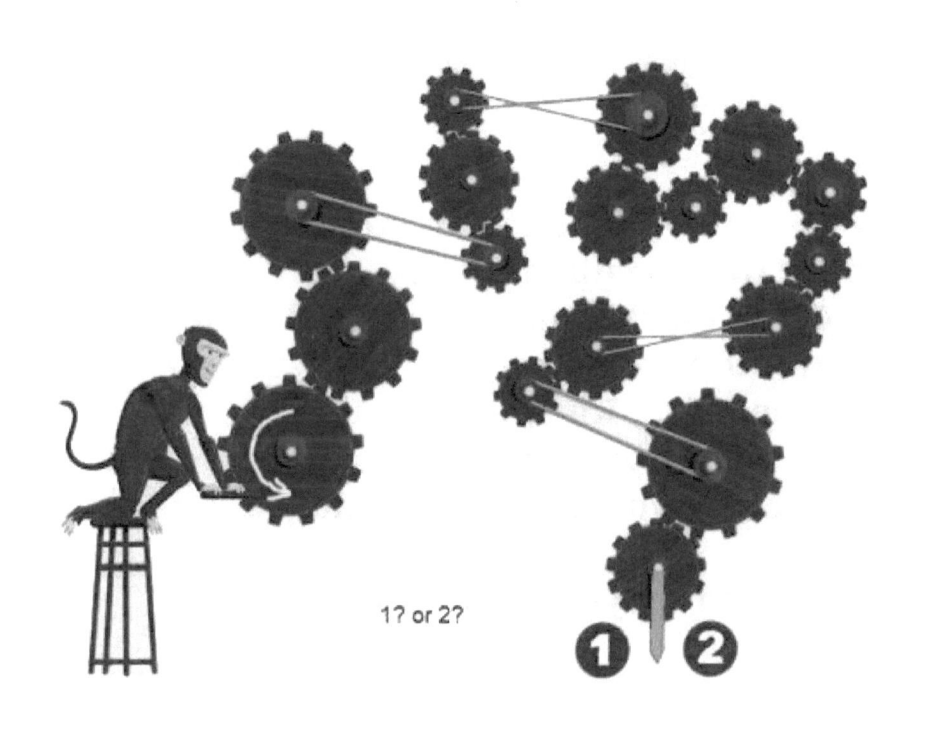

Will the Pointer Move to 1 or 2?
- 2

- Summary

88

Below is the banishing spell. For each riddle/puzzle the players solved they were given 1 of the lines of the spell. 6 riddles/puzzles and six lines of the banishing spell.

1- For thou who slept in stone and clay, heed this call, rise up and obey.
2- Come on through the mortal door and show yourself once more.
3- Rise, Rise, Rise, RISE!
4- You are now banished to air and sky ...
5- Forever you shall float and we will not sigh.
6- Up and up you go .... Good BYE!

The staging for this next event is much more advanced than other parties. Once again, I used my backyard pond. Well before the party I found a clown doll at a local thrift store. I had meant to take some pictures of the doll after the party, but my dogs got to it before I had a chance. Picture below is the same doll, just not the actual used in the party. Mine looked much more aged. I also drew meaner eyebrows on with a Sharpie.

I attached the doll to a fishing string and sunk him in the pond. Fishing string went up and over a high branch that was conveniently above the pond. That was attached to a point not accessible to the kids.

The pump that normally drives the waterfall was hooked up to a remote outlet and the hose was left disconnected under that water. This was similar to Ghostly Treasure, Sample Game Five, in using the pond pump to churn water for effect.

The clown I bought had long red hair, so I cut a bunch off and spread it around the pond. I also made little handprints from non-toxic paint and put them along the rocks, where the clown 'crawled' into the pond. Most of the kids did not notice any of the hair or the handprints. So I had to do the old "Hey, what is that??!!" to bring those clues to their attention.

Once the players were all gathered around the pond, they started the chant. When they got to the "Rise" part, I clicked the remote I had in my pocket and the water began to churn. When they finally yelled "BYE", I pulled the fishing string and up from the water 'floats' the clown and up into the trees he goes.

To my chagrin, what I had envisioned as the thing of nightmares, the kids thought was more funny than scary ... Either way, fun was had by all, but maybe next time I'll have to rent some scuba gear and really give them a scare ...

Seed Ideas

Since the beginning of this book I have run many more successful kids' parties. The kids always had a great time, learned a lot, and created memories that will last a lifetime. Just recently my high school age son, who has an interest in chemistry, remembered the experiment that resulted in 'elephant toothpaste' we did years ago. He is interested in trying it again, on a much larger scale …

There are lots of opportunities for other story baselines that could lead to great learning opportunities. Here is a list of a few seed ideas I have had that would be fun to try:

- Spy vs. Spy – Have two teams of spies trying to outwit each other to find the location of the top-secret plans. Both teams have same sets of clues, but it is a race against time to see who can solve them first. This is definitely on the more competitive side and would be best suited for older kids.

- Assembly Required – This one would take some planning and know-how, but would be awesome and adjustable for any age group. Also, you can't get much more STEM than this activity! A set of construction plans would be part of the hidden clues. The parts to assemble whatever the item is, for example, water balloon catapult, water-rocket and launcher, etc. would also be hidden around, with possible hints to their location. Once they have the plans assembled and all the parts found, they can try and put together and test/use the device. This can also be an item that was bought and disassembled and needs to be put back together using an assembly diagram.

- Play the Play – This one could be lots of fun for extroverted kids and be hysterical for the audience. Chose a play, an easy one or even create one of your own, based on the type of party or make it more confusing by having the subject of the play, be the play itself. Have various costumes or costume parts hidden about. The costume found is the character that the player must assume, or they can create it based on the parts of the costume they find. Now have the script of the play be the clues. The main objective is to figure out how the clues go together forming the scripts of the play that then must be acted out. If they figure out the correct order, the play will go smoothly and make sense. If they do not, it should be pretty funny. They will need to figure out the logical progression of the play.

- Mystery Meal - This would be one that can take place entirely inside, but with a small group. There would be a list of ingredients available and recipe clues broken up into various pieces. For example, each recipe is now in three pieces. Add a few extra ones and put them in a box. Kids will first need to match up potential 'good' recipes. All the recipes should either be relatively simple or be close enough to avoid different oven temperatures and times for example. Having recipes that do not involve cooking is another option.

  Each recipe is broken up into a list of ingredients and directions. This would make each item easier to divide up into clues. Imagine taking two of these recipes and making each ingredient and direction a separate clue mixed up in a box. If the kids do not figure out the correct combinations, it will lead to some quite interesting creations.

  Here are a few examples that might work together well, variations of these recipes can easily be found online:

  <u>Chocolate Chip, Peanut Butter and Banana Sandwiches</u>

  Ingredients:
  1/4 cup creamy peanut butter
  2 tablespoons honey
  1/4 teaspoon ground cinnamon
  1/4 teaspoon sugar (optional)
  2 tablespoons miniature semisweet chocolate chips
  4 slices whole wheat bread
  1 medium banana, thinly sliced

  Directions:
  Mix peanut butter, honey and cinnamon (and sugar)
  Stir in chocolate chips.

Spread over bread.
Layer two bread slices with banana slices
Top with remaining bread.

Peanut Butter Pop'ems

Ingredients:
1/3 cup chunky peanut butter
1/4 cup honey
1/2 teaspoon vanilla extract
1/3 cup nonfat dry milk powder
1/3 cup quick-cooking oats
2 tablespoons favorite cereal crumbs

Directions:
Combine the peanut butter, honey and vanilla in a bowl
Stir in the milk powder, oats and cereal crumbs
Shape into 1-in. balls

Apple and Peanut Butter Sandwiches

Ingredients:
4 Medium Apples
2/3 Chunky or Regular Peanut Butter
Fillings (Granola, Chocolate Chips, Cereal, Candy …)

Directions:
Core apples.
Cut each apple into slices of desired thickness.
Spread peanut butter over slices
Sprinkle with fillings of your choice
Place additional apple slices on top

    Themed parties are also fun with younger age groups and can be the central focus of the party, or just an added-on bonus. So many options here as well: Pirates, Princesses, Knights, Dragons, etc. There are so many more opportunities if you go outside of the typical storybook type characters. Go with team Thomas Edison verse Team Nicola Tesla in a race to develop electricity or prove which is better AC or DC current. What about Claudius Ptolemy with his earth centered model verse Nicolaus Copernicus with his sun centered model. Switching gears and leaning more into the arts with team Salvador Dali verse Man Ray (Emmanuel Radnitzky). You can explorer art, books, movies, etc. The options are endless.

Wrapping Up and Moving Forward

Since my kids are older now, we have moved on from the mystery parties to doing a very involved Haunted Yard during the Halloween season. We set up a walkable maze in our yard and use animatronics, friends that are scare actors, lots of decorations, lights, sounds, etc. This takes a lot of time to plan, design, set-up, and execute, so the mystery parties for the kids, as well as the adults, have been put on hold.

That being the case, opportunities are always there. Almost any type of party can be an excuse to incorporate one of these mystery games for any age. Birthday, Housewarming, Wedding reception parties, etc. Any holiday would work as well. For example, who stole all of Santa's gifts!? How about a retirement party that tracks all the retiree's accomplishments and future endeavors?

For more advanced situations and using the same concepts, parties could be created for Bed and Breakfasts, Companies, Family Reunions, etc. I know that at least one Bed and Breakfast has used my first book to create murder mystery parties and recently I was contacted by a company to potentially create a mystery party oriented around their workplace, possibly posing as an inspector, and of course finding something 'wrong' and needing to track down the culprit. Being a teacher, I can also see how I could incorporate some of these gaming techniques into my lessons to make them more fun and engaging. Possibly running a mystery challenge over a few days of class.

As always, the only limitation with these parties is your imagination. So, go forth and create something memorable, educational, and most of all fun! Good Luck!

Feel free to test your skills with this end of book clue.

42/1/15   21/1/1   1/1/17   49/8/2   5/4/18   30/1/18

Made in United States
Troutdale, OR
06/24/2024